by Tom Clark

Airplanes (1966)
The Sand Burg (1966)
Stones (1969)
Air (1970)
Green (1971)
John's Heart (1972)
Blue (1974)
At Malibu (1975)
Fan Poems (1976)
35 (1976)
How I Broke In (1977)

WHEN THINGS GET TOUGH ON EASY STREET

SELECTED POEMS 1963-1978

TOM CLARK

SANTA BARBARA
BLACK SPARROW PRESS
1978

12/1978
Am Lit. Cov

WHEN THINGS GET TOUGH ON EASY STREET: SELECTED
POEMS 1963-1978. Copyright © 1978 by Tom Clark.

The poems in this book were selected by the author from the follow-
ing volumes: *Airplanes* (Once Books), *The Sand Burg* (Ferry Press),
Stones (Harper & Row), *Air* (Harper & Row), *Green* (Black Sparrow),
John's Heart (Goliard/Grossman), *Blue* (Black Sparrow), *At Malibu*
(Kulchur Foundation), *Fan Poems* (North Atlantic Books), *35* (Poltroon
Press), *How I Broke In* (Tonboctou Books).

Chicago and *Suite* were first published as Sparrow Chapbooks.

Some of the poems herein also appeared in the following magazines:
Angel Hair, Anon, Big Sky, Chicago, Clear Creek, Eye of the Wheat-
field, Frice, Granta, The Green House, Grilled Flowers, Io, Little
Caesar, Lodestar, The Nation, The New Yorker, The Ohio Review,
The Paris Review, Periodical Lunch, Poetry (Chicago), Poetry Now,
The Quarterly Review of Literature, Quixote, Rolling Stone, Sailing
the Road Clear, Stooge, Sun & Moon, Thrice, Wild Oats, The World,
The Yale Lit., Yanagi.

LIBRARY OF CONGRESS CATALOGING IN PUBLICATION DATA

Clark, Tom, 1941-
    When things get tough on easy street: selected poems 1963-1978.

    Cloth edition limited to 226 signed copies.
    I. Title.
PS3553.L29W5   811'.5'4   78-13630
ISBN 0-87685-348-3 (paper edition)
ISBN 0-87685-349-1 (signed cloth edition)

Dedication: *A True Story, for Angelica*

One night in the summer of 1966
I was sitting on the balcony
Of a small mountain cottage
In the Maritime Alps

When either the sky suddenly cried "Poet!"
Out of the very depth
Of its hidden sonorities,
Or I naively so imagined it.

And in the deep blueness of that evening
And in the million stars
Pinned to it, I thought I saw the design
Laid out for me by

My destiny, and I bowed to it:
It would be hard
To take, but like a ballad about
The death of a beloved sung by a guy

In a gorilla suit, it
Would have its lighter
Moments, too. You would be one
Of these, or perhaps all of them.

TABLE OF CONTENTS

1. 1963-1967

2. 1968-1972

3. 1972-1976

4. 1974-1978

1.

1963-1967

A DIFFERENCE

Something fallen out of the air, some
thing that was breathing there before
stopped: or say it is a difference

felt quickly on turning from one's work
to the window, and seeing there the same
trees the same color, the sky still without clouds,

changed only in reference to the trees
which also seem to have turned away.
The world still external but less distinct

at its center. For a few
seconds. Fall. The centerfielder drifts under
the last fly ball of the summer, and puts it away.

THE KNOT

"l'homme n'est qu'un noeud de relations,
les relations comptent seules pour
l'homme"
                                                —St-Exupéry

The four of
them together
beneath the roof
of the one
room school—

some one's
relative
is in the photograph—

in my hand
it breaks, a leaf
found in a book,

the yellow veins, the brown
split edges. I

Imagine them—the four

together—holding
hands; all are

dead now. A man
is his relations
with men, he

is strings
coming together

to form a knot,

who
has had a hand in it.

A WINTER DAY

A winter day, thirty degrees
in the sun, cold

sunset. To say
a flower in a glass

is like the sun, begs
the sufferance of the thing, the

sun. It has been so many times
compared. Instead

to say
today, a winter day

we picked a willow spray,
put it in a glass,

studied the setting out
of its branches.

Thread and fold of the willow,
thin cloth drawing off

your hips and breasts
as you stooped to touch the glass,

and a sufferance
argued, in your eye

suffering my eye to follow.

SUPERBALLS

You approach me carrying a book
The instructions you read carry me back beyond birth
To childhood and a courtyard bouncing a ball
The town is silent there is only one recreation
It's throwing the ball against the wall and waiting
To see if it returns
One day
The wall reverses
The ball bounces the other way
Across this barrier into the future
Where it begets occupations names
This is known as the human heart a muscle
A woman adopts it it enters her chest
She falls from a train
The woman rebounds 500 miles back to her childhood
The heart falls from her clothing you retrieve it
Turn it over in your hand the trademark
Gives the name of a noted maker of balls

Elastic flexible yes but this is awful
You say
Her body is limp not plastic
Your heart is missing from it
You replace your heart in your breast and go on your way

CHANGE

Stepping down was like being born
out of the flank
of a bus, like Dionysus from
Zeus. The guts of the pavement
lay open under flags and gazers.

As we passed the bank and needle,
still on the bus, you gazed
out and then it seemed I was Dionysus
and you Diana or another in the bays.
I rushed toward you as if Zeus
heard you when you turned to me, amazed,
and said "It's strange to see the world through
your arm."

YOU (I)

The door behind me was you
and the radiance, there like
an electric train wreck in your eye
after a horrible evening of waiting outside places in the rain for you
    to come
only to
find all of them, two I know, the rest scullions, swimming around you
in that smoky crowded room like a fishbowl
I escaped from, running away from you and my André Breton
dream of cutting your breasts off with a trowel
and what does that matter to them or to you now, but just wait,
    it's still early
to the children embroidered in the rug, who seem to be setting up siege
engines under a tree house full of midgets who look like you.
Where are you in this sky of new blue
deltas I see in the drapery, and your new friends wearing bamboo singlets
what are they doing down there in the moat waving tridents like stalks
    of corn?
Me, I'll be happy to see their blood spilled all over the bedspread
pavilions of your hands as an example. If you come home right now I'll
    scrunch your hat
between my thighs like a valentine before you have time to wipe them.

YOU (II)

You are bright, tremendous, wow.
But it is the hour of one from whom the horrible tremendousness
Of youth is about to depart.
The boats are ready. The air is soft and you perhaps nearby
Do pass, saying "I am for you."
This is as much as "everything is great."
But desperation builds up all the time.
Life is nothing
              more to me
Strapped at the bottom
      of the throat
Than majesty, I think. You are arduous as that
Ashtray. Swallow me! since
Your hands are full of streets
And I walk out upon the streets
And I think the girls are better looking, vicious, cool
And the men are flying kites and newsprint
Gets on my arms. I enter rooms—
Wild my steps like an automaton's—
Where batons are linked into some residue.
A gull is eating some garbage.
The sky is an old tomato can, I think.
I buy a newspaper and begin to walk back.
Smells torture the kites like gulls. Wild gulls, and
It's the tremendous sky of survival.
Few things are still visible to me. Baseball
Withholds the tremors. They fall, so
I drag you down and
You are akimbo as I stick it in
And everything is thunderous accordion April, great,
Risen from palms and hypnotism. I run home
And dip my coffee in bread, and eat some of it.

YOU (III)

Today I get this letter from you and the sun
buckles   a mist falls over our villas
with a hideous organic slush like the music of Lawrence Welk
I lay in bed all day, asleep, and like some nocturnal
beast. And get your salutation among the torn green numbers
in the sky over the council houses. And see your eyes when
                                        the retired pensioners pass
me by the abandoned railway station—this is not nothing, it is not
                                                        the hymn
of an age of bankrobbers or heraldic days but it is to sing
with complete gaiety until your heart freaks. I love you.
                                  And go down amid the sycamore

summer. Wandering by the lake any way
                        seems lovely, grand, the moon
is a gland in the thigh. Tumble and twinkle as on the golf course app
lifts. And a door is opened to
an owl. It is snowing, and you are here on the bed with me
and it is raining, and I am as full of frets as a guitar or a curtain
and I am singing, as I sponge up the cat place. You
                                are heaped
the word reminds me of Abydos and spinach. A curtain
of belief keeps me away from the tombs
of imagery. I love you, I'd like to go.

YOU (IV)

the chords knotted together like insane nouns   Dante
you are in bed   in the dark copula you
of the musical phrase   a few star birds sing in the branches
their voices are tangled not high
now all of them are dark and some move   you
were a word, in the wood of my life
where the leaves are words, some of them fucking
in obscurity their clasping is terrible and brusque
pain birds ache thru them   and some
are lighter and seem to suggest less
of death than of a viola da gamba player these
birds sweep past in the forest
of my hands on your chest,   as we move
out on the glowing sea of the tropics on an ice pack,   you,

YOU (V)

O Earth Mother, who consents to everything, who forgives everything
don't hide like this   and tell
Her Power is sweetened in these rays, the Earth before her
        conceals the children
of her breast in her cloak, meanwhile we feel her,

and the days to come announce
that much time has passed and often one has felt
        a heart grow for you inside his chest
They have guessed, the Ancients, the old and pious Patriarchs,
        and in secret they are, without even knowing it,
        blessed
in the twisted chamber, for you, the silent men
but still more, the hearts, and those you have named Amor,
or have given obscure names, Earth, for one is shamed
to name his inmost heart, and from the start however man
when he finds greatness in himself and if the Most High permits,
he names it, this which belongs to him, and by its proper name
and you are it, and it seems
                        to me I hear the father say
to you honor is granted from now on
and you must receive songs in its name,
and you must, while he is distant and Old Eternity
        becomes more and more hidden every day,
take his place in front of mortals, and since you will bear and raise
        children for him, his wish
is to send anew and direct toward you men's lives
when you recognize him   but this
directive which he inscribes in me is the rose
Pure sister, where will I get hold, when it is winter, of these
flowers, so as to weave the inhabitants of heaven crowns
                        It will be
as if the spirit of life passed out of me,
because for the heavenly gods these signs
of live are flowers in a desert   I search for them, you are hidden

20

THE LAST POEM (after Robert Desnos)

I've dreamed so much of you
Walked so much
Talked so much made love to your shadow
So much that there's nothing left of you
What is left
Of me is a shadow
Among shadows but 100
Times more shadowy than the rest
A shadow that will come
To rest
In your life in which the sun
Is so much.

MOMENTUM

I saw the busy street you crossed the last time I saw you
as the river of time, carrying you away forever.
Your pale coat was swirling like a leaf in the current
in the crowd of anomymous bodies hurrying back to work.

I turned around and started to walk in the other direction
but because of the tears in my eyes I failed to see a dentist
standing outside the entrance to his office and collided with him,
knocking him down.

DOORS

A love that is not pardoned
But burns the hand that touches
The wind
Tears her form out of the corner
Something presses me her voice
Across the sea a light is lifted
A woman walks to the edge
Of the mud in the street clinging to her packages

In the car of the sea these rusted shapes
Take up the night with a music like stone
The door will not close
Smoke   The cotton
Stuffing of the room
Flatness under my feet walking around the room
A weight on my tongue
The stone fenders are close to the water
At any step you might fall
Things are going badly now
Nothing swims up through
The metal that holds the muddy flowers

There is dirt in every space and a cold wind
Comes off the sea
Pleats of the bedclothes make a hole in the light
And the wall bends up losing you
As far apart as it can go
Breaking into pieces like a bird

We go at different speeds
Side by side while you sleep

It is grey ahead where I am going

It is too hot
All rooms beat constantly

Something is the matter with the doors but no one stops
We rush through the joys that were there
The same weight of confusion leads me
To pick up everything I find
I turn this over in my hand and find you
Your hands are behind your head
Forming a grave on the pillows
Reality only listens when your words are true
How much longer can the door be found
By picking strings
To a chamber where a vestment
Never speaks until the door to the other side
Upward through the mud to the spoons
Has been closed
A chorus of swine lets loose

In a grey corner the rats continue to sing
Most of this is useless
An insane need for genuflecting
The night flaps
I stand at the edge of you
Is there a switch to be turned
To end this bluff against music
Which outshines the diamond in the slush
All of us wanted to have
Are there green parks where bicycles still glide
We sat on the hills quarreling

As you undress the perfection
Of hair marking each part of you
That seeps down through
This maze of pictures
I carry like sections of cloth *d'or*
In ancient painting there is a duel in which
There are
Wings beating in something like hay
Beyond which the mystery is encountered again
She replaces the packages under her arms
And walks through the door

EYEGLASSES

Of this house I know the backwindow
lodges six housesparrows in the bricks

Under the sill, and they are the birds
scour these roofs all winter for warmth

Or whatever. Two are arguing now
for a few inches of position on a cornice.

How the mind moves out and lights on things
when the *I* is only a glass for seeing:

I stand at the window

Setting down each bird, roof, chimney
as the boundaries of the neighborhood they make.

I have on an old blue jersey.
Every two hours I wipe off my glasses.

THE LAKE

1

Poets, do not sneer at everything
A tree is like organized crime
It spreads its roots everywhere
When you sing of a tree
You sneer at justice   Goodbye, Lake
Poets! The radio is chinking out
Caprice Espagnole by Lao-Tree

There's not much beauty here
Just a speck, a crumb
That's fallen on your dress
From a table full of ugliness
Look, on this small speck
I will subsist like a coot
In my cornflake nest

2

The horse in the picture
Has two legs raised high   He is
Waving to someone   Probably
A lady horse   You are so beautiful
In my mind because you are not
A horse   The farmer takes a wife
He sits upon her torse
And creates little farmers
And farmeresses   Then he goes out
For a ride on his horse   Lady,
I ride straight to you
Like a line out of a geometry
Book   Madonna! Lady of Mythic
Motions, Lady of Mondrian, Lady of the Lake

3

I like timber art   There's lots
Of it here at the lake
Above the timber there are snows
And above that, a wolf
I write you long letters
From my cabin here by the lake
Where I write late

Long poems and letters
From a lone wolf
Who likes you
And hates art
Like this lake art
The snow creates on my breath
With its wolfish flakes

4

I have several pets
Among them a wolf
And a horse   A legendary lumberjack
Created them for me
With a hoisting apparatus
Whose strong beams
Move deep in the lake

My pet, my legendary dreams
Of you among the lumber
Of this ordinary lake
Are distant as a wolf
And skittish as a horse
But out of them I hoist
You, my love, my pet creation

5

Some disorganized *concerti*
Are skidding across the house
Like a horse skidding
Across the ice on the lake
The arm is far from sturdy
It makes zigzag lines
On the apparatus

No one can cross the snow's arms to
The distant timber
Lines of creation, for beyond
Them nothingness lies
Like a wolf and waits with death
For the horse, and its ordinary
Rider to cross the lake

6

Lake Life, I want to take a bath
In you and forget death
Waits at the muddy bottom
Although I live in the tree
Of poetry and sing, I have no
Water wings
And fear death by drowning

Sometimes I get a pain in my breath
Apparatus, then I stop breathing
Long enough to count the trees
Across the lake, and the leaves
Whirling on the water
Start to sink slowly, in circles
That down deep, become straight lines

THE LAKE: CODA

Last night I dreamt I saw
Your face in the lake   I hid till
With the sun the small
People in the lake awoke   And shook

The dew from their silk jackets
Aloft to flowers and grasses
Like a morning lamp, and swept
Sleep from the woods with wings

Like tiny brooms   Until the ways
Of the minor world glowed
With traffic in each inch, and day
Rung from pool to hilltop like a bell

You live with the pale and weak
And meek ones in the mud
To whom the keys of the air are given
And lights rising throne on throne

AFTERNOONS

It's fine to wake up and hug your knees
my knees
when I have run out of fire fluid
I rush back to bed

the feeling of paws on my knees
petals and wings
little hair,
why have you gone

I sing that in my head
being alone is a song
a cigarette in bed
it's better not to touch the ceiling
but if love attaches a band-aid
from the ceiling to your head
there's nothing to do but recognize it.

SUNGLASSES

The air is interesting
My sunglasses today.
Last week they were

Interested by the sea.
In my sunglasses
I look like Grandma Moses

Wearing sunglasses
And interested by the sun,
The air, and the sea.

How hungrily
She looks at the world
Today!

Is it a child's wisdom
In the colorful pine tree
That throws itself upon Grandma Moses?

On her back she fades back
Into the sandy land
And changes slowly to silicates.

How interesting she seems
To my sunglasses
Who cry "O Daughter!"

POEM

My heart in pieces like the bits
Of traffic lost in the blue
Rain confused I roar off into
To learn how to build a ladder
With air in my lungs again
To be with you in that region
Of speed and altitude where our bodies
Sail off to be kissed and changed
By light that behaves like a hand
Picking us up in one state and putting
Us down in a different one every time

HITCHING

In the photograph in which (just as our drive is starting) we notice that
There were six families in Barking
Six husbands and six wives (the caption explains that
Now in 1966 they are all alive),
Some children have entered the picture.
One of them may become champion of the world.

I'M ON AN ISLAND

Do not try to adopt me
I am not a pigmy soothed
Boy or baby hitchhiker saint

What is wrong suddenly
Is that I swallow a cold
Blast of air, I mean fright

Spill coffee on my book
And hear the kinks
In the great universe

The warp in the coffin
Phantom men fly out of
Anywhere in this world

POEM

Like musical instruments
Abandoned in a field
The parts of your feelings

Are starting to know a quiet
The pure conversion of your
Life into art seems destined

Never to occur
You don't mind
You feel spiritual and alert

As the air must feel
Turning into sky aloft and blue
You feel like

You'll never feel like touching anything or anyone
Again
And then you do

2.

1968-1972

UP IN HERE

All her aroused feelings
   pour through a hole
      changing from particles to waves
    of noise to bury every signal

You chop your way out of the vocal bush
      using your cane for a pool cue
         Now the shot
      the word pops into place
 bing!

You are passionate but afraid
     to fuse someone's mood
   the "you" that is asleep
   to the "she" that is you   a model
    of light and logic
      but you do

A pledge of allegiance to the mobility of the day
   where a bird lights on a branch
 like a beautiful song lighting on itself
   to bring you grace

AIR

The sweet peas, pale diapers
Of pink and powder blue, are flags
Of a water color republic.
The soft bed, turned back,
Is a dish to bathe in them.
This early in the morning
We are small birds, sweetly lying
In it. We have soft eyes,
Too soft to separate the parts
Of flowers from the water, or
The angels from their garments.

THINGS ABOUT YOU

1

I write this for your eyes and ears and heart
If it makes your eyes sore
ears weary
and heart burn
Stop!

I come to things about you
I didn't use to understand

I didn't mean to use you
I just summoned you

Then at the end you are soft and bent
The way a tulip is droopy a lilac is not

knowing this
is a joyous experience
for me
gives you endless pleasure

You are casual when others are only easy
You go directly toward your own thought
There are some things about you I don't understand

that's why I married you

Do you think these are banal thoughts?

that IS what it's all about
the portrait for instance
of the *inside* of the surface of something

The way *You Didn't Even Try* is "about"

Do out and in exist?

and up and down
are lies about them

2

Did you say something?

THE SINJERLI VARIATIONS

1

Had it of come my way
I'd of had it.

2

It'd of come
had I had it my way.

3

Way off, it had come.
Had I had it?

4

Had it of had my come
it'd of had it.

5

I'd of had my way
had it of come off it.

SLOW LIFE

1

Cinematic blossoming of love gasoline

2

Blue windows behind the stars
     and silver flashes moving across them
   like spotlights at movie premieres

long cool windshield wiper bars

3

the butterfly gently opens itself like a fist
     dividing into wings   and drifting off
       over the cube's puzzled head

NIMBLE RAYS OF DAY
BRING OXYGEN TO HER BLOOD

After the sponge bath
Spice cake and coffee
In a sky blue china cup

Tiny clouds float by
Like bits of soap
In a bowl of very blue water

A happy baby sleeps
In a silky chamber
Of my wife's lovely body

A leaf spins itself
The leaf's a roof
Over the trembling flower

Everything's safe there
Because nothing that breathes
Air is alone in the world

The kaleidoscope
of evolution winks at me mysteriously from the
baby's face in ways that stomp on understanding

MAGIC ARRIVAL NO. 7

Not less because in purple I descend
The western day through what you called
The loneliest air did you arrive at what you are,
A unison of every fragrant thing yet brief
Like the perfection, after rain, of the color
Blue, its clear articulation in the air
When it and the sun suddenly come in the room together

CROWS

Like the shore's alternation of door   wave
Shoe   wave, the displaced and disturbed
Air replaces itself with more air as casually
As attention grants itself, and I observe
Two crows sew themselves onto the lace flag
Of that flying cloud, whose cosmetic grace
Adorning the Plain Jane face of the day
Pins them in an unlikely halo of pale light
After one blast of which they dance away,
Croaking shrilly as abandoned divas
Whose black scarves flap in the breeze
Over every home and panorama, dark precise
Signs washed up on the air to be noticed
Out of a continuous process of succession

NOW SHE DWELLS HERE

It was the work of fortune
which brings joy and not pain only.
But can a winged thing become less?

She lived on E. 75th Street
to speak plainly.

I mean: in the divisiveness of love
two people pass through
the same instant separately

for all their awareness sighs
for life and not for each other
but in doing that it does.

ONE

Light spray over a daisy chain of days.
Many wives, brought on rocking boats,
Dissolve in one loved damsel.
Jury of sighs, it is Time
To load the back with groceries
With my brother and my wife
Because life is a family.
Did I drive right? Risky slopes
Deer start across, hushed timber
Cool and the engine smoking.
When mouths of fog cover the truck
Pushed by wind, the ocean sends
Us violet shrouds, bears
Brush us in the dark eucalyptus.
Where the hawk dives, a flowing zone
Lights the road. A brown head whispers
In the restless advance of trees
And cars, friends of lonesome men
In the brunt of a huge wave.

PILLOW

Our arms sleep
Together under water

Air curves into the room
On feathers

Apple leaf light
Beneath the blankets

A butterfly of hair
In the breeze

SKY

The green world thinks the sun
Into one flower, then outraces
It to the sea in sunken pipes.
But twisting in sleep to poetry
The blood pumps its flares out
Of earth and scatters them. And
They become, when they shine on
Beauty to honor her, a part of
Her laconic azure, her façade.

THE GREEKS

Deep in the air the past appears
As unreal as air to the boy
Or the apple of the world
To a girl whose eyes are pale and mild
Her hair is probably not real gold
Only a very good imitation of the Greeks'
Like a map of that world of early days
Where woman lives on a scarlet cloud
While man in colorless blunt noon
Splashes up at the blue variables
That pass by on an airplane of words
Into the sky which distributes gifts of
Rain and light over our lives equally
Infinite gifts we are unable to behold

WHISTLE BUOY

That grey droning note
  I've heard every dusk

Neither owl nor foghorn
  but similar to both

The low fluted "day-is-done"
  of some unknown warbler

Atonally breathy memo
  of universal mysterioso

Tucks misty roses away
  in the dark's soft envelope

Safe under a lion's paw
  of starry numerology

Whose silver figures
  fleck the surf's Afro

Otherwise sparkling brassily
  into the liquid air

BLOBS

Green ink (stars)
           fly hurriedly over these pages
                     so white
           like pianos at the North Pole
                 and make them a lovely
                 leaf-colored room

for the Oriole
to live in
           & also

    other animals, the fox
the pumpkin spider whose gossamer we . . .
               the shark & pelican
                   the elk, the moth
the world of the tropical fish
      & give them (don't fence them in!)

           pre-nonlinear television

           & the adult monkey . . . uh, he
has coffee
   while this is going on; wildly
he thinks: "you're trying to
steal my spinal power, holy shit!"
                 for he is nuts
           so that

now there are holes between
               the unfielders
   where unseen powers may pass

the dope.   Out of the baggie a hologram of
           the cat steps up to the plate
           where there is oil left,
                 cucumber oil

                in a Swiss cheese universe . . . What

did you say?

"A mile or two from here, in a grove
of eucalyptus trees, monarch butterflies
from all over California gather, once
a year, to hustle a little ass," she say.

                        But let us somehow
leave it—this populous niche—
                        behind us
                        momentarily, and travel
                        through the lettuce of the 5th dimension

into the brain of Phil Whalen, in reality
a circus of tiny electrical events no more
difficult to catalog than the connotations
of *Hamlet*.
                A charming space, motherly
                                where
"Blue mice ride neon bicycles" in & out
of the woodwork,
                &
                        the blue
spots on the belly
                        of the red fish
                change color, drastically
                like

                new models.
The elk lock horns in staggering combat to evolve.
                But when
                the eggs
                        are hatched, later, &
under a gnashing sky
                        the babies stream out,
                        making their painful statement
                                of Love,

what good does it do the doe?

LIFE NOTES

Like a big tired buffalo
                              or ox
Mount Tam kneels beneath
                    a glittering ceiling
her blue and green
                    flanks rest, her shaggy
head settles
              and drinks from the lagoon.
The fur of her underbelly is burnt and brown
cars wind down in it
                      like ticks. The top
of her head is yellow and balding
except where a few squiggly redwood tips
crest it. She rests, in the blazing
light of a June afternoon, as I do.

Life is not conditional. IF
is only a
            half-life.
A Whole Life—yours, mine, its—
can pass by in an instant. Hers
continues, like a music without notes,
unless you really strain
your ears to hear them, and maybe even then.

NOTHING INSIDE

People on television
give you their
public self

like people
on elevators

TV

Nothing inside
a space
the surface of which
is filled
with tiny messages

MORE

More hair
every
day

HEAVY

for Jack Kerouac and Charles Olson

When the gods die
the myths
are lifted off our backs.

Peace be with them.
They were heavy.

INTO

even the
perfect
jumpshot

can't match
the perfect
pass

for insight
into the
mysterious

AFTER AMOS OTIS

Marvin Gaye sings *Trouble Man*, comes apart
Moves down the line a token interest
Ray Davies sees space as famous
But the only stars I know are in the sky

The moon is in the second house
Jupiter aligned with Mars
So I go out by the herbarium
And puke on a moss rose

I'm beginning to see the light
It's looking black & blue
My stomach's in knots
No longer grateful to be white

"There are problems in these times
But ooh none of them are mine"

HOT DOG

I am watching Mouse Factory with one eye
and my other eye is on Warren Jabali
who steals the ball and drives bravely
and at half time a returning POW (black)
admits he'd like a piece of the pie
but they'll probably be giving lumpy gravy
laced with the snow white pacifier
that'd keep even King Kong in line
the Greeks gave it credit for wonders of nature
which by the way applies to this here Julius Erving
who lopes in for a backward slam while I blink
then glides upcourt like a Clipper Ship

THE DOOR TO THE FOREST

for Jim Carroll

Eric Dolphy can't wake up:
the green light's still burning
by the gate. Pine cones

when stepped on by
dogs or raccoons, click
gently, like bones

into the mist, which
smells like mint; the
sounds diminish it;

the white fire rose
through the dropper's eye
falls; and the rain remains.

A SAILOR'S LIFE

Whatever interest
there was in
difference's gone.

*

She rolls the sounds
around and around.

A piece of speech
falls out of her mouth.

*

"A peace
of speech,"

says Ginsberg.

*

Like the Big Note
of which all music
is the resonance
is the poetic sentence.

*

You're a piece
of the same person
I'm a piece of.

*

Who is Lewis?
Who is Joanne?

*

What'd Ed Sanders
call Bolinas—
a psychedelic
Peyton Place?

*

"The locale of this book is
California, and the Californian
will find much in it that is
familiar to him; the characters,
however, are imaginary, as are the
situations; and, in one instance,
a whole neighborhood."

*

The "Democratic
Response" to
Nixon's
State of the Union
Message—

Speaker of the House
McCormick,
80
years of age,
can't read
his lines
on the teleprompter

*

Other
places to go—

Aspen

67

Santa Fe
San Diego

(Go ride the music).

*

My wife's
birthday—
February
5th.

*

Visitors
in 1969:

Too many
to name.

*

After the rain

camelias
bloom too soon.

*

half silver
half black
eucalyptus leaf

*

2 FROM STRANGE DUDES

Imitation of Ted

Suede vest

68

over blue sweater
over brown shirt
& tough white chest.

When a man's
in love,

he's riding high above
whoever'll hold still for it.

Imitation of Ron

Betty!
To touch your cunt
in the car—was this
too much to ask?

Did you have to break
all the fingers of my right hand?

*

Virginia Slims
Jimmy Miller

*

"Turn My Life Down"—
that was
last summer—playing
on the radio again now.

*

By the sea,
by the sea,
by the beautiful
sea

*

Reading the California
poets—Rexroth,
Patchen, and Meltzer

*

Spent this winter
thinking, writing,
getting sick, and
watching basketball.

*

My one strength—
my women
are behind me.

*

tape   pop the tab
loop   pinch the roach

*

"Because everything flows in the direction
of least resistance, and because the heat
to the south was too great and likewise
the cold to the north, the least resistant
direction was approximately west"

*

satellite photos
of the weather
as God sees it
& easy does it

70

*

follow the downstream flow
to the store—difficult
hitchhiking—the winter
of Charles Manson

*

Q. (TV reporter): "Doing better today?"
A. (Manson): "Always doing good—everyday's better."

*

finding   Bill's Erik
a 4-leaf clover   Satie
in the grass   notebook

*

KMPX plays
"Peace Piece"
by Bill Evans

*

Planet News

*

O Speech, tell me if
our brothers and sisters—
the other breathers—
are safe in here with us.

*

A place where
the time of the year

71

is a color—
dark green.

*

Favorite songs
of 1969:
"Wooden Ships"
and

"A Sailor's Life."

3.

1972-1976

AT MALIBU

Kowabunga! The amoeba was
                          mountainous.
Venusian burgers were sailing out
         of broken windows
                          onto my plate. The Fantastic
   Baggys were playing.
                   Down on the corner
           of Tubular Boulevard
     and Transistor-in-the-Back-of-the-Head Avenue,

                   near the approach
to the Gaping Maw Freeway,

              the 6-to-8 plus
                   foot waves
         were coming in like gangbusters
                   out back of the
                   Bar-B-Q Shack.
         Jan & Dean
                   & the Rip Chords
         were playing
                   on portables
         in the All-Nite
                   Board Shoppe;

         chill were the shakes
         and flat the tops.

A blue Merc cooked out of the light.

                        The cars were lined up
                        like igloos
                        in front of the
                           Tastee Freeze.

   Greasy smoke was

rising from the
Taco Bell, much as from
the La Brea Tar Pits.

Placid grew the mucoid
plugs of the beauty contestants.

"I'm bugged at my old man."
"Trig pisses me off."

They were listening to
Danny & the Juniors
on incredible car radios
that picked up 1962.

The history majorette
in the Sting Ray
wore a locket
with a tiny picture
of the La Brea Tar Pits

'tween her round blond
boobies.

She waved & winked
as I walked across
the parking lot
of the Howard Johnson's.

Paul Revere & the Raiders
were vooming
out of the tape deck
of a Land Rover
on the entryway.

Soon,
gleaming up at me
from a chinawhite plastic plate
was the oily yellow mucilage
of a machine-fried egg.

Then a spatial cliff
          loomed up before me
     like a breakfast of grey rock

     and spanked my ass.

     I vommed up a string
of what looked like bird shit,
          and cried out
     to the ripped-up air:
"What Me Worry?"

TO KISSINGER

The amoeba is mountainous Hank!
It dwarfs yr think tanks you neoid!
So jack off my octopus!
I don't care if you did make it with Barbara Walters of the Today Show!
Hit the deck 4 eyes!
The meat train won't be late for the grave and you're on it!
Jelly arms are coming for you across the black glyphs!
The cellophane is crinkling!
Earmuffs won't be enuf!
You big donkey made out of orlon!
Spirochetes et yr Mom!
Ach Nein!
When the storm of time movies hits the protein sources
Popeye'll take you one-on-one you shell of Frankenstein!
You'll climb off the food chain soon enuf anyhow Henry!
The gods of death live in yr shoes!

11/5/72

CHINESE FOOD

Staring at the plate of strangely dislocated Chinese food
As it travels away from me
Diminishing speedily in a far off violet dimension
I suddenly realize
If a point in space doesn't exist
Then its coordinates don't exist
That's how it is in logic
But here on Earth
It's not so simple to eat off mats
Because
As the sock falls off the foot
Toejam is apparent
So
I toss back
A chili dog
And a bottle of coke
And I feel like
Hank Aaron

I aim the ice cream cone
At my mouth
But by accident it
Ploops
Into my forehead

Then I do my harmonica act
On a cob of corn
And suck up
A couple of big slabs
Of watermelon
Seeds rind & all

A powerhouse
Hums inside my body
In a tremendous surge of meaning
Like having Burt Reynolds bring out a copy of my latest book

On the Johnny Carson Show

Scratching my ass I leap into the Wax Museum
Still clutching the soy sauce

AUTOBIOGRAPHY

Through the meat market
of life
I have dragged
my white ass
for 34 years
without looking back
at the butcher knife
as it whistled past
dividing
my hairdo
into 2 parts

Tom Clark
man of pain
you need a lie
to make you brave

and you need the truth
to make you
come off it

THE STARS

No one sees the insane shining
Spaces where the stars pass
Time by drowning their aloneness
In the high of the truly deep

GOODBYE

Hey
Earl Butz
poetry
is the humanoid
fire
that leaps up from
the
drunken flower

When
I scrape up
as little as
one phrase
from the nothingness
it gouges out
a hole
you could drive
the Abyss through!

BREADWINNING

The Hound of the Basketball summons me
With a sort of scarlet thud
As blood passeth before my eyes
And I realize it's time to arise and go
To the school
To shoot a few hoops
In the saffron air of twilight

I drive in for a layup worth 50¢
Reminding me that
My agenda still includes
The acquisition of bank notes
Sufficient unto the purchase of foodstuffs
And transportation of the items so obtained

What Wordsworth called "getting and spending"
Meaning to pass money through space
In a circulatory repetition I find tedious
Tho it does have a tautological beauty
Like the reincarnation of victims in cartoons

It's odd to live on a rubber band like that
So off I go to the post office
And send mss. to New York
Whence grammar tries to force itself on me
And bend me into a spectator of life
But I run off down Mesa Road to the silver tanks
Punching the air and hollering things
Piltdown Man would understand

And on my way
I am leapt upon by a slavering collie
Whom I beat back with blows of a rolled up shirt
Much as in time of crisis one harks back
To Australopithecus

For when grunts proceed from this form divine
And drool at the corner of its mouth rudely gathers
Then may one perceive its actual origins
And the bush-browsing Homo Erectus is recollected

So I get on the mental trolley and ride homeward
Wondering if
Any more chores remain
Like large holes
In the side of the Trojan Horse jello mold?

The words are massed there
Deeper than my probes may go
Tho I have given them
A Frankensteinian energy
Still I am not surgeon of happy tunes that shake the walls
So I must chop through the mush
To where the earthlings are waiting to be fed
And put to bed

They receive the package of hot dogs with happy chirps
And day is done
And this is good
For now I have permission
To fuck off

BASEBALL AND CLASSICISM

Every day I peruse the box scores for hours
Sometimes I wonder why I do it
Since I am not going to take a test on it
And no one is going to give me money

The pleasure's something like that of codes
Of deciphering an ancient alphabet say
So as brightly to picturize Eurydice
In the Elysian Fields on her perfect day

The day she went 5 for 5 against Vic Raschi

CLEMENTE (1934-72)

won't forget
his nervous
habit of
rearing his
head back
on his neck
like a
proud horse

THE GREAT ONE

So long Roberto Clemente
You have joined the immortals
who've been bodysnatched
by the Bermuda Triangle

When your plane went down
it forced tears out of grown men
all over the hemisphere
Al Oliver and
even Willie Stargell cried

You had a quiet
pissed-off pride
that made your countrymen
look up to you
even if you weren't
taller than they are

No matter how many times
Manny Sanguillen
dove for your body
the sun kept going down
on his inability to find it

I just hope those Martians realize
they are claiming the rights to
far and away the greatest rightfielder
of all time

TO CLEMENTE IN SEPTEMBER

Watching the season die on television makes me think of you. Roberto,
   in the end
Your despair willed itself up in a bitter threnody, like mine.
They tried to root the both of us in temporality, Johnny Heidegger-style.
It turned out not to be that easy. I declined outright, losing my rights
   to money.
You said, "Look at my *statisticos*. They are pure number, out of time."
The sportswriters looked at you like you were crazy.

                    Around 1969 you became more personable
But harder to pin down. You started to read all that watery poetry
Known as the handwriting on the wall. Your back hurt. You were 35.
   Even so
You hit .345. The next year you hit .352. But you seemed to know
Neptune would soon claim you. You faced the humans, but only
With your eyes turned aside toward the divine animalia
Were they swam. Angels the size of dolphins pulled up at your door
   and said, "Let's go!"
They were as big as Chevrolets but you did not want to go. You hadn't
   even said goodbye
To your family!

              The backs you ride into space won't mind your weight,
   Roberto.
You always kept yourself in good shape, and besides, isn't gravity on
   the fritz
These days? When a creep like me survives? My wife reminded me of that
Between innings. She's lovely; maybe you remember her from my poems?
I only wish you weren't dead, Roberto, so you could get to know her.

89

AND YOU ARE THERE

Wearing the familiar Yankee pinstripes
With the heraldic 𝕹 elegantly covering the heart
over a longsleeve white sweatshirt
Babe Ruth sits on a hardback chair in front of his locker
It is locker No. 3

The photographer has caught him in the act of
Reaching across his body with his large and powerful right hand
To untie his left shoe

His long slim legs in black knee socks are crossed
And his body hunches forward over them
With his left hand dangling in his lap

His head is moon-shaped and seems much too big for his body

He cocks his head up to the left as if someone there is speaking
His eyes are intelligent and wary
His nose is broad
His ears are enormous
They are pinned back flat against the side of his head

In its cowish amplitude his face
Slightly resembles Severn Darden's

The Babe is saying something we can't hear
To a person whom we do not see
Probably a reporter since the whole scene looks strictly posed

Three doors down the row of lockers
On a Persian strip rug
Which covers the board floor of the clubhouse
There is a pair

Of two-tone Oxfords—brown and white?—
The kind golfers used to wear

Maybe they're Wally Pipp's

90

INTERESTING LOSERS

for Bill Veeck

Although I had felt many emotions
The meaning of the word "pity" remained
A mystery to me until 1951
When at the age of ten
I discovered the St. Louis Browns

Then
For three short years
A more pitiable spectacle could not have been disclosed

At first base the Brownies had Hank Arft—no kidding—
At second who but the unmemorable Bobby Young
At short the scrawny yet not untalented Billy Hunter
At third a variety of persons including the unsung Fred Marsh
And the washed up Vern Stephens
Who hit the highest popups
In the entire universe

In left field grazed the confused but impassive Dick Kokos
Whose visage lay inert in my mind until one minute ago
When I remembered that baseball card from around 1950
Which showed
A beautiful aerial view of Dick Kokos swinging
Or rather
The conclusion of his swing
Which seemed to involve Dick in a strange state of contortion
Whereby his bat having achieved a 360° arc
Came around and hit him in the back of the head

Meanwhile in center field there was the baby faced Polish hopeful
Johnny Groth
And in right the handsome rapist Jim Rivera who perfected the kamikaze slide
Not to mention the deep thighed Don Lenhardt
The insouciant George Schmees
Or the pretentious Jim Pisoni

Ah and the Brownies had some great pitchers
They had the wee Ned Garver who somehow won 129 games
The ageless Satchel Paige who was meant for something better
The fiery Virgil Trucks
The bitter Lou Kretlow
The ravaged Gene Bearden
The pissed off Tommy Byrne
The useless Bob Cain
And the deteriorating Ray Coleman

And behind the plate
And the greatest of them all
Was scrappy Clint Courtney
Who couldn't play worth shit
But was so tough
He once swallowed an old jockstrap full of rusty nails
For a promotional stunt
Between losses of a doubleheader

That's what's called a St. Louis Browns Taco nice going Clint!

SON OF INTERESTING LOSERS

Eddie Gaedel came from Chicago

In 1951 he was 26 years old and stood 3 feet 7 inches tall

Bill Veeck signed Eddie Gaedel to a St. Louis Browns contract on Saturday night July 18, 1951, the night before a big doubleheader in Sportsmans Park against the Detroit Tigers, a Sunday doubleheader celebrating the Golden Anniversary of the American League

Veeck's promise of a holiday promotion brought out better than eighteen thousand people

Nobody was disappointed or surprised when the Browns lost the first game to the Tigers

Between games, members of the ground crew wheeled a huge birthday cake out onto the field, the cake had 50 candles, one for each American League season

The midget Eddie Gaedel stood at his full height inside the birthday cake, wearing his white St. Louis Browns home uniform, with the number "⅛" on the back in brown

Eddie was nervous it was dark inside the cake

When they got to home plate the bearers put the cake down and knocked on the side to let Eddie Gaedel know it was time to come out

He came out

The crowd cheered

Bill Veeck, the one-legged war vet, wearing his famous open-neck sports shirt, grinned from the press box

The second game started

While the Tigers batted in the first inning, Browns manager Zack Taylor
    helped Eddie Gaedel tie his shoelaces in the dugout

Eddie's hands were shaking

The Tigers finished batting and came off the field

Carrying a tiny kid's bat, Eddie climbed out of the dugout and
    approached the plate

He informed umpire Ed Hurley that he would be a pinch-hitter for the
    Browns' lead-off man, Frank Saucier

Hurley stood apart from his mind for a moment and took a second look

Gunfighter-fashion, his strike hand shot back to his pants pocket
    Where it got a good grip on the rule book

Zack Taylor loped out of the dugout to show Hurley Eddie Gaedel's
    official contract with the St. Louis Browns

The mists of time cleared from the umpire's eyes

Eddie Gaedel stepped into the batters box

Bob Cain, the Detroit pitcher, wound up and fired

The ball exploded into the catcher's mitt a foot above Eddie's head
    for ball one

The next two pitches blasted in high and wide of Eddie's tiny strike zone

Bob Cain swore softly and spat into the grass in front of the mound

"Shit," he thought, and then he threw the softest pitch he could throw:
    Eddie never saw it: he had his eyes squeezed shut

"Ball Four," said Hurley

Eddie Gaedel trotted off to first base

Immediately Zack Taylor replaced him with a pinch runner

The next day the American League banished midgets from its playing
fields for all time

League President Will Harridge ordered that Eddie Gaedel's statistics
be erased from the record books for all time, and it was done

Bill Veeck paid Eddie Gaedel a hundred bucks

The Browns went on losing, Zack Taylor's hair kept falling out,
Bill Veeck split, the Browns went off to Baltimore and became
winners, and Eddie Gaedel got bookings on the after dinner circuit

Over meat and potato leavings he told the fathers of high school
letter winners about his day in the big leagues

Years passed

In the late 50's Bill Veeck got back into baseball with the Chicago
White Sox

One day he called Eddie Gaedel and asked him to drop by with a couple
of his pals

Veeck dressed the four midgets up in plastic outfits to look like Men
from Mars

Then he hired a helicopter and had it circle over the infield at
Comiskey Park

Eddie Gaedel and his fellow Martians came down the sky ladder and
landed at second base, where they captured two White Sox infielders
at raygun-point

It was like a St. Louis Browns Reunion!

TO BILL LEE

Spaceman, how was your trip to Peking?
I hear you didn't have such a great time
and you're off to a terrible start
this season
with an earned run average of 12.12 per game
having given up 26 hits and 11 walks
in your first 16 innings
which is a hell of a shame
because when you're not doing well
the reporters don't like to talk to you so much
and when they don't talk to you I don't find out what you say

It could be when you're going this lousy
you don't say much anyway
I wouldn't blame you
but don't worry
the season's still young
I know you're not
I don't mean I know you're not young
I mean I know you're not worrying
because as you've said many times
for example after Tony Perez hit that painful home run off you in the
    Series
you'll still be alive tomorrow
barring a traffic accident
or cardiac arrest

You are of a philosophical cast of mind I know
even though you are a little temperamental those two traits can exist
    side by side
I mean I have seen you stomping around in the dugout
and screaming at umpires as though you wanted to kill them
but I also know you've read a lot of serious books and have many
    interesting thoughts
such as about whether intelligent life exists on other planets
and about Pyramid Power, of which you are a devotee

96

and about the Bermuda Triangle, which when you told him about it
        Bernie
Carbo thought you were talking about pussy, and told his gorilla so,
and also about ginseng, which you use before you pitch
the way Popeye uses spinach
before he saves Olive Oil by punching out Bluto, and of which you are
        thus an exponent,
and about Eastern Religions too
after many years of inquiry into which
you've concluded that techniques of wacked-out meditation
can be applied in the practical field say
so that for instance in your best example
a Tibetan priest could make a baseball disappear
and then materialize again down the line in the catcher's mitt

"There," you say, describing it,
"is my idea of a relief pitcher"

You're telling the truth, as usual
and as usual all the writers are
cackling like you were doing standup comedy

You're also telling the truth when you say that people don't generally
        realize how hard you really work
How for instance you're always one of the first guys to get out to the park
How you help set up the batting cage
How you shag fly balls and run a couple of miles every day
and how you actually work on catching ground balls behind your back
because you have this theory that because of your exaggerated
        follow-through
you have to

Remember the time you tried your theory out on the late Don Hoak?

It was in 1968 at Winston-Salem in the Carolina League
You were a cocky punk just out of USC
You gloved a ball one handed behind your back
That play started a game ending twin killing
and it also made Don Hoak, then your manager

97

want to kill you
Hoak chased you all the way to the bus screaming his head off
and when you got on
he stayed outside, yelling at you and pounding on the window

This is your life, Bill Lee, was not what he was saying

Don Hoak never understood you, Spaceman
It wasn't in the stars
Don's nose was just too hard, I reckon
He couldn't conceive of people like you and Hans Arp
who hurl the truth into the bourgeois face of language

People like Reggie Smith and Pudge Fisk
will never understand you either
because you tell it like you see it

You told it like you saw it that time with Ellie Rodriquez
and lost a few teeth for it
but what are a few teeth in the face of the truth?

You tell it like you see it in Spaceman language like your spiritual grandfather Picab
even when it gets you into hot water
like it did last summer when you shot off your mouth
about how you thought Busing was a pretty good idea
and about how you thought the Boston fans
who disagreed with you were bigots with no guts

Those contentions were sensible enough I grant you
and I happen to agree with them
but then it's easy for me, I don't have to pitch in Boston
and you do and did
and it wasn't easy last summer
for although you were in the midst of a fine season
the populace was growing weary
of your smart remarks, your blooper pitches
and behind the back catches. Tibet
and Pyramid Power never did
interest Sox fans much, so that when
on May 20 you shut out the A's

with a quasi-spectacular one-hitter
no one seemed to notice,
the response was merely polite,
no one seemed to understand how well
you were pitching, how no lefthander
to put on a Red Sox suit
since Mel Parnell
or even just possibly
the legendary Robert Moses "Lefty" Grove
had pitched quite as effectively
and consistently
as you were doing;
it was as though everybody was just waiting for you
to fuck up.
And you kept on
not fucking up.
On July 27 your unique sinker was never better
than in a 1-0 masterpiece over Catfish Hunter,
the breathtaking parabola of your blooper ball
never more tantalizing or bizarrely elongated.
But still you were not approved of
as you would have been had you not been
funny in the head. You began to speak
curiously after victories.
On August 9 you beat the A's again
and afterwards said they looked
"emotionally mediocre, like
Gates Brown sleeping on a rug."
What did you mean by that?
On August 24 you beat the White Sox 6-1
in a downpour at Fenway. It was one
of your greatest days. At one point you fielded
a ground ball behind your back by sticking
your glove up over your left shoulder,
spearing the ball, and from a sitting position
starting a double play that ended up with
you lying flat on your back in front of the mound.
Still, when it was over, you sensed the contempt
of the writers and fans. They loved you
but they did not love you. "When I'm through,"

you said, "I'll end up face down in the Charles
River." Spaceman, why did you say that?

That was your seventeenth victory
the third year in a row you'd won 17 games
and this time it looked like
you had a good shot at 20 or
better. Little did you know you'd go
through the playoffs, the Series, the winter
and the first two months of a new season
still looking for that next victory. Or
did you know, and is
that what you meant about the Charles River?

You had arm trouble, sure. Then Johnson
kept you out of the playoffs even though
you'd beat the A's twice and called them
emotionally mediocre earlier. In the Series
you pitched well in the second game
but Drago lost it in the ninth. After
the infamous Fisk/ Armbrister non-obstruction dispute
in Game Three you said that if you'd
got to ump Larry Barnett you'd have "Van
Goghed" him. You meant you'd have chewed
his ear off? Johnson scheduled you
to start Game Six. "It's not often a
mediocre pitcher gets to start in the
sixth game of a World Series," you said.
(You turned out to be right.) When someone
in the gang of writers asked you if this
was the biggest game you'd ever been asked
to pitch, you said, Nope, this is nothing
compared to the 1968 College World Series.
"That was real baseball," you said. "We
weren't playing for the money. We got
Mickey Mouse watches that ran backwards."
And then when someone else asked what you'd
do if you won and forced the Series into
a seventh game, you said you'd declare an
automatic 48 hours of darkness so Tiant

could get another day's rest. "That's what Zeus
did when he raped Europa," you said.
"He asked the sun god, Apollo, to stay
away for a few days."
                    The next
three days, it rained. Apollo, perhaps
hearing your words on a Tibetan wavelength,
split, and not only did Zeus favor you
by washing out the sixth game, which was set
back from Saturday to Tuesday—he ordained
Tiant to pitch it. And you were pissed
off with Zeus and with Darrell Johnson. You sulked.
But when Carbo's pinch homer tied it
in the 8th, I saw you climb up on the rim
of the dugout and wave out toward the left field
wall, where Carbo's ball had gone,
urging your teammates on. Four innings
later, Pudge Fisk's homer over the same wall
won it for Boston, and you danced in the
dugout with the other Sox,
happy as in Frank Lima's perfect phrase
a bunch of fags in Boystown.
                    That left
the seventh game up to you. You pitched
your ass off, serious for once, and took
a 3-0 lead into the 6th, but then Pete Rose
busted up a double play by banging into Burleson
and up came Tony Perez. I know you hate
me to mention what happened next but it's
a part of the story, Spaceman. You tried to
float your blooper pitch past The Dog
for the second time in one night. That was
once too often, like Tony said later.
You thought you could do it;
you were gambling; that's why
they call you Spaceman. They call
Perez The Dog because he persists. "I saw
him all the way," he said later; "I was
ready for it." Boom! The ball
disappeared into the screen. Two runs. An

101

inning later you came out with a blister
and a one run lead that was gone by
the time you hit the showers. So much for
Tom Yawkey's World Series Dream. You
sat in the locker room with your head down
amidst your sad teammates later. "I just
went out there and did my job," you said,
in your disappointment using the cliché for once.
"I went out there and threw the shit out
of the ball." The blooper ball you threw
Perez? "Hell, I live by that pitch
and I'll die for it," you said half-
tragically. This time nobody laughed.

And then you left for China.

1976

TO BERT CAMPANERIS

You've had your problems
over the years but when
the money's on the table
you come out smokin', Campy

You didn't have to go through all this atavism, you know

You could have stayed home and made lariats in the rope factory like
    your father
but you went away to the big leagues
for $500
and on your first time up even though your English was bad
you hit a home run
and that made Charley Finley happy
and after he made you play all nine positions in one game for a joke
he made you his shortstop for life
meaning until your legs start to go
which I hope isn't soon
since I love the way you play the field
with a cool mechanical glide
and intensely run the bases
so diminutive and severe

We're both 35
and you're earning 100 grand now
and looking for a five year contract
and I'm getting a hundred bucks
for doing this poetry reading

Which I guess just goes to show
how good you know English
don't count for everything

CHICAGO

I

I leaned back against the wall and laughed a crazy laugh.
I punched myself in my face with my fist, combed my hair,
And made it out the door to the El station.

It was a hot summer day in 1955.
Heat waves jumped off the El tracks.
From the train you could see down into the backyards

Of dingy flats on Lake Street where angels lived in dejection.
Ragged looking wash hung there: grey t-shirts w/o arms.
Next came vistas of wrecked cars and the bolt factory . . .

Downtown I changed trains for the North Side.

*

I wear khakis, a white shirt, blue tie.
I carry a leather bag containing my uniform.
I enter the park through the players' gate.

It gives me a kick to do this.
It means I am not only getting in free
But possibly creating in passersby

The mistaken impression
That I'm a bigleague ballplayer!
Since I'm just 15 this seldom happens

But when it does it's dynamite! Sometimes—once a week or so—
Some schmo who's either unselective or overeager
Even asks me for my autograph! Outasite!

*

Once inside the park, however, I bust my ass working . . .

104

In Comiskey, there's an usher's locker room under the 1st base stands.
At Wrigley, it's down the leftfield line almost to the bleachers . . .

I go in there and put my uniform on.
Other ushers are dressing around me. Some of 'em are old.
Most of us are under 18 and six feet tall or more . . .

Most of us go to high school, or used to,
In the Catholic League, as I do. Most of us are tough!
Most of us live on the South Side, but I do not. Most of us are Irish.

All of us are white. One dude shows up for work
With a perfectly rectangular laceration on his forehead
Where he got hit by a brick at the dance last night: "I never felt it!"

Everybody puts his uniform on and goes in to see Andy.
Andy has his dark glasses on. What he says goes!
Sometimes it's his son Andy Junior. He also has dark glasses.

Andy Junior is married to Miss Florida no less.
Andy Junior's wife is the greatest thing
To hit the usher's locker room since baloney sandwiches!

I'm working in the third base boxes at Wrigley Field.
It's a hot day. In my head, I sing "Volare".
The wind is blowing out toward the lake . . .

The vines are green. The grass is green. The sky is blue.
The Cub uniforms are white. The wind blows.
In batting practice even Eddie Miksis homers.

On the scorecards there are the Wrigley gum cartoons.
The cub scorecards are lovely. So is Ernie Banks.
P. K. Wrigley is away at Catalina.

P. K. Wrigley's wife sleeps the endless sleep.
P. K. Wrigley's wife is in a coma. Does she dream of Ernie Banks?
P. K. Wrigley has a motor launch on Lake Geneva.
Every Labor Day, P. K. Wrigley takes his boat out for a spin . . .
And the Cubs never win the pennant with Ernie Banks.

*

The Cubs have Bob Ramazotti, Roy Smalley, Eddie Miksis
And Wayne Terwilliger. No wonder they lose all those games!
I don't give a shit anyway, being a White Sox fan.

I cheer for all the opposing players in my heart.
I work by the visitors dugout one day the Pirates
Are in town and have a chat with first baseman Dick Stuart.

Dick is a young player at the time. Later they will call him
"Doctor Strangeglove," for he hits home runs but has iron hands.
This disparity of gifts has not yet come to haunt him:

We talk openly for a few minutes
About the pussy situation in various towns
A subject on which Dick is a little better versed than I am.

Another day, Orlando Cepeda and I shake hands . . .

*

Wrigley Field is day baseball retirement-sunny.
Comiskey Park is on the South Side . . . a different story.
Orestes Minoso's go-go intensity is magnified by the smell of blood

From the stockyards. One midnight
After an extra-inning game against the Yankees
I'm walking down 35th Street toward the El

When I step into this scene out of Dante:
A saloon lit by some grisly aura of rosé
Out of which a screaming black woman

Virtually explodes! Bursting
Through the double doors of the bar and out into 35th Street
Clutching one hand to her chest

And screaming . . . I think what the fuck

And then I see it . . .
She's holding one of her tits on with her hand!

Somebody just cut one of her tits off
And she's holding it on with her hand!
Jesus Creeping God!

*

I meet a girl at Wrigley Field. Sob.
She's sitting in my box.
She has a platinum ponytail.

She's wearing plaid bermudas. Her legs are tan.
During the game, she spills
Some popcorn

On her lap.
Involved in the game, she doesn't notice.
The popcorn moves around

When she does; some of it
Scrunches right down into her pussy!
I feel incredibly envious of it . . .

Later I chat her up.
Her name is Cathy or something.
She lives somewhere like Elmhurst or Wheaton.

We ride home on the Northwestern together.
But I get off at Oak Park
And she keeps on going

To Elmhurst or Wheaton
And I never see her again
Because due to my excitement

I am completely unable to remember her phone number
Even though I have carefully memorized it!

At Sox park the drunks are fantastic.
They charge the field, throw beer cups, pee in the aisles.
If the crowd's big enough, pandemonium

Is always present at least as a potential . . .
One Saturday the Boston Red Sox are in town.
A million kids are here to see Ted Williams.

Their dads are all happily smashed . . .
Then in the seventh inning, a fat and mean
White Sox pitcher named Harry Byrd beans Jim Piersall!

Piersall crumples to the ground! It's the real thing.
He rises, dazed . . . looks around . . . suddenly, he charges
With his bat swinging and a wild yell

Proceeding from his throat as evidence of an intent
To cause Harry Bird's immediate demise!
But his berserk charge is completely zigzag

So before Piersall gets to the mound, players and coaches
Of both teams have arrived; a huge fake brawl
Ensues, allowing Harry Byrd to escape with his life.

The fans, taking theater for reality, are stunned
Only briefly. Then one or two maniacs
Leap the low walls and sprint directly into the fray.

One giant dude in my section waves
A toy gun as he rushes down the aisle toward me . . . I step back
As he goes by. Spit is running out of his mouth.

At this point, I glance out at the field and notice
That Ted Williams, alone,
Is standing in the Boston dugout.

With one foot on the step, he stares down at his perfect hitter's hands.

II

Day dawns with great predications of clarity
And analgesic love. I drive to the beach
At 7:30 and lie on the sand reading Emerson

While over the Michigan side the sun's
Fireburst-red T-Bird smokily ascends . . .
Emerson tells me me and the sun are one

Kind of poetry plucked from the Big Soul's harp
Of which all solid things are the strings
Or something . . . Transcendence I get hot

When I think of you! Not to mention Nietzsche
Or Jack Kerouac, or even The Big Bopper!
Voluntary starvation equals insanity achoo!

I stare at each grain of sand inquisitively
Waiting for Old Eternity to roll me
A boulder or two out of its heavy hopper

Like Beethoven told me it was supposed to!

*

Dale Bonga picks me up before daylight.
We drive to the golf tournament.
For ten hours we keep the fairways clear,

Inspect tickets and direct parking,
Run errands conveyed via walkie talkie
From the clubhouse, and see to it that

The groupies don't pester Ken Venturi too much.
For three days of this we make 40-some bucks,
And Ken Venturi makes twenty-two grand.

*

The racetrack's a great gig to get assigned to regular.
Regular ushers work the owners' boxes.
The owner of a winning horse is inspired by largesse

And a few drinks; in the throes of victory a tip
Of 50 bucks—or a fistful of win tickets—
Isn't uncommon. But whenever *I* get the track

It's as a replacement, for a day or two only;
From my post in the grandstand, I can barely
Make out the money as it flashes from hand

To hand, two hundred yards below me. *My* tips
Come from fetishists who want to stand in the aisle
And other hunch artists to whom some suspension

Of the standing-room rules is worth six bits;
Also, from the grandstand runways, it is
Frequently possible to shoot some terrific beaver

During the races, and this speaks in the grandstand's favor.

*

The weirdest gig of all's at this museum
On the South Side near the Lake. It's actually
The decaying once-private home of a wealthy family.

Decades before, it had been an attractive mansion
In a fashionable part of the City. This was
No longer the case. However, the house remained

Open to visitors, on Sundays only,
For the exhibition of various junk
Such as suits of armor, stuffed birds, duelling pistols,

Third rate European paintings, and so on . . .
It never occurred to us as ushers to wonder
How all this stuff came to be there,

110

But there it was. On a typical Sunday of super-tedium
Perhaps 7 or 8 people happened in
To view the relics. My customary post

Was in a small room, off the main halls,
Containing several tapestries imitating the Cluny originals
And a harpsichord. There was also a phonograph

On which a recording of Bach harpsichord music played.
My job was to see to it that the record kept playing, over & over.
Also, I guarded a stairwell which led down

From the tapestry room to a small dungeon, faintly lit,
In which stood a naked mannequin wearing a Medieval chastity belt,
The sight of which was regarded as dangerous to youngsters;

Accordingly, I was to permit
No one under the age of 18
To gain access to this stairwell.

*

Among other things, hiring goes on at the Office.
The Office is on West Madison Street near the Chicago Stadium.
Outside, hoboes carry wine bottles in paper bags

As they shuffle along to the distant tune of some
Jimmy Reed 45. Inside, the ushers hang out.
There's pool tables, a kind of clubhouse thing.

Doors lead off to inner offices. I go through one.
In the boss's inner sanctum Andy checks me out.
I pass the eyeball test without a word. Obviously

My background is on my side. Good cop blood! OK,
They take me out & fit me with a uniform
And tell me I start tomorrow at the Furniture Convention.

*

The Furniture Convention's at the Merchandise Mart.
It's easily the worst gig in my two years as an usher.
I direct creeps from the chair and table trade

On & off elevators from 7:30 to 4:30, for three days,
Accumulating equal secretions of chagrin & boredom interiorly
Until my brain feels like a compost heap in Grand Rapids . . .

Everytime some fat jerk asks me where to find the hoors
I suppress my pre-beatnik sense of social outrage
And tell him how to get to Wells Street.

*

Third Balcony at the Chicago Stadium defies fantasy.
Its denizens are capable of every heinous act.
Stabbings, even abortions, take place during hockey games.

Blackhawk fans hurl pennies and eggs onto the ice.
The pennies and eggs immediately freeze over,
Leaving small bumps upon which it is hoped

Opposing players will skate, tripping dangerously.
But hockey fans are angels compared to the folks
Who show up for boxing. At the Robinson-Fullmer fight
      (May Day 1957)

I'm working in the Third Balcony. Fights, of course,
Erupt bloodily all around me; it's not my job
To interfere, only to report deaths & serious woundings;

But this time something hideously untoward occurs:
A fellow in my section pushes another fellow
Over the railing! The last I see of the latter

Is his legs, pointed straight up, Icarus-style, as he falls . . .
It takes me several minutes to realize
There's no real reason to report this, since it's

Now the responsibility of the usher in the
Corresponding section of the Second Balcony,
Directly below . . .

*

Taking tickets for football games at Wrigley Field
I freeze my fingers off one too many times
No fingers left . . . I QUIT!

*

Working on the field at Bears games
I stand next to Big Daddy Lipscomb of the Colts one day
And lose all my illusions of being tough forever.

*

Wrestling at the Amphitheatre
And Roller Derby at the old
Arena on South Wabash . . . now there's

Two scenes so weird you'd need
Claude Levi-Strauss, with slides by
Hieronymus Bosch, to clue you

In on 'em—not me.

*

So I'm working at the Amphitheatre one summer night
And it's a heavy card: Gorgeous George himself
Versus this French dude something like Charpentier

And the morons are going crazy, lapping up the camp
And acting like the fake uppercuts are actual
And spilling the wet popcorn down the back of their necks

Due to waving the popcorn box up in the air, etc.
All very much as usual

Except for one thing: a terrific storm's going on outside

And the lightning's flashing at the emergency exit doors
And the thunder's rocking the building
And word's going around that all the South Side viaducts are closed

Because of flooding . . . which turns out to be the truth
So that on my way out after the show, ducking big drops,
I dash past stalled cars lined up behind the viaducts

Making it to the El station, and I catch my train
Downtown, and change for the West Side
But the storm's worse now, and the El line's blocked

At Austin Boulevard, the tracks are underwater,
So the passengers get out and walk, but the streets are
Underwater too now, cos the gutter drains are blocked

By jammed-up leaves and newspapers, the water's hip deep at Ridgeland
I'm wading through the dark streets with my bag above my head
To keep my uniform dry.

*

The uniform: you saw it on TV at the 1968 Convention.
Blue coat & pants & hat, with trim of white & gold,
White shirt, blue tie, shoes optional

Which doesn't mean you don't have to wear shoes
It means you wear your own shoes
As long as they're the right kind of shoes, black

Oxfords, or brown oxfords, not (for instance) sneakers, or loafers,
Or again, ski boots, nope, nor
Open-toed sandals, baby booties, high heel pumps, my God!

Fur-lined and covered mukluk boots, snowshoes
Boat shoes, deck shoes, track shoes, galoshes
Ballet pumps, slippersox, Ace bandages nor tape—none of those are allowed!

*

Things to do when you're an usher:
Show people to their seats
Be ingratiating and hope for a tip

If it's raining, wipe the seats off with a rag
Then smile ingratiatingly
And hope for a tip

Take tickets before the game
Count tickets during the game
Stand on the field after the game

Watch for people (especially kids) who're sitting in the wrong seats
Chase them away unless they look like they can pay for it
If they look like they can pay for it, make them pay for it

Solve disputes among the paying customers
As long as they aren't *too* mean or drunk
Always using the personal rule that discretion is the better part of valor

Look busy even when you're not (remember Sartre's Waiter)
Learn how to rest while standing up
Keep an eye out for the secret dicks who spy on ushers for the Boss

Keep an eye out for the chief
Keep an eye out for the beaver
Keep an eye out for the coffee break

Keep an eye out for the foul balls during batting practice
Run the kids off the balls then grab them
And sell them back to their dads for 50 cents (the balls that is, not the kids)

Work at the American Legion Convention and feel inspired
When you're permitted to grasp
Harry Truman's fishy little hand

As you escort him from his limousine through
The Chi. Stadium players gate (same gate Bobby Hull uses!)

115

To the great hall where Legioneers sit with programs in their laps

Who listen enthralled then, as Harry the T lays down his famous rap
About how he went to bed and had a good night's sleep
After ordering a nukeburger to go

For the entire population of Hiroshima

BIRDS

Sky full of blue nothing toward which the Magi
Move, like dream people who are Walt Fraziers of the air . . .
Sometimes the moves they make amaze them
For they will never happen again, until the end of time; but there they are.

So shall I be like them? I don't think so . . . and yet to float
Above the rolling H_2O
On wings that express the mechanics of heaven
Like a beautiful golden monkey wrench
Expresses mechanics of earth . . . t'would be bueno

I WAS BORN TO SPEAK YOUR NAME

I knew the tune
It was my song
Even before you came along
Yet only then did I perceive its meaning

This *you* I wished for
This desired Other of whom
I spoke so glowingly in poems
I never knew its name

When I lifted its arms up
I noticed tiny wings
That's all I knew
The rest was Muselike
Anonymous this "you"

So I guess those poems
Were like phonecalls to the future
I think I had your number
Knew what I was looking for
Even before I found it
In the face directory

And luckiest of all
Your human substance
Was life's loveliest
Far as I could see

As if I'd placed
Bones and skin
Together in a dream
You were put together that way
But I wouldn't let it go to my head if I were you

EVERY DAY

Awake the mind's hopeless so
At a quarter to six I rise
And run 2 or 3 miles in
The pristine air of a dark
And windy winter morning
With a light rain falling
And no sound but the pad
Of my sneakers on the asphalt
And the calls of the owls in
The cypress trees on Mesa Road

And when I get back you're
Still asleep under the warm covers
Because love is here to stay
It's another day and we're both still alive

*

You're sleeping with your hands
Between your legs
And your hair blown back
Across the pillow
Like a mane

The more times you sing to me
From the mare's smoothness
Within your body cavity
The less lost I feel
When I walk past the dead people

GIFT OF TONGUE

It's Christmas Eve and I run in the sun
There's not much holiday traffic on Mesa

A VW goes by with surf board sticking
Up through the roof like a shark fin
A girl on a black horse says "Hi!"

Christmas trees line the center of Brighton
Kids went to the city and got em
One of em's even covered with real snow

So goodbye to another year and I don't know
What to make of it though I'm fairly
Sure it won't be money
I'm pondering that seriously

When you come down the stairs in blue velvet
Like a long cool drink of water viewed
Through a prism of purest ultramarine
And all of a sudden I can speak English

SUITE

1.

Got to be there, so that she'll know
when she's with me she's home. On
the air waves across the nation
energy imagines it can move that way.
But sleep hides her modes as nature's.
Her skin is a dreaming surface—
blood drifts up through shadows,
light shifts on minimal rubies,
the spots on water where fish breathe . . .
impossible to see them coldly
or in some numerical epitome.

2.

What the picture tells me is itself.
Now I know how to go on:
hold still, dry your eyes.
Life is actual, warm and near
and completely without character
except for the melodious enigma
of her body and the possibility
of monkeying around with it immediately.
Otherwise, the room contains only
a metal writing table, a chair,
a flower box, and *The Corpse* of Balthus.

3.

The tones of voice are petty
for a while, then change to affection
then quiet is disclosed like
a jaguar running on damp grass
and the heartfalls converge for an
instant at speechless thunder now.
Neither knows whose limbs are whose,
or whether they are those of automata.
For a moment the ocean reaches in the window
and painlessly strangles consciousness
with a sheer cloth—a pair of ladies' hose?

4.

Then again by day fog drapes the boats
off, blocks the bouquet of the sea
wind, and creates vertical cathedrals.
The muscles turn to slop
or the extension of something electrical.
Then the chemical thing stops
happening. Anger's the logical product.
It explodes softly in heroic attitudes.
Breakfast looks black and your thumb hurts.
The clouds are scratched and used.
The pump isn't working. The purple
light spins around and around, very slowly.

5.

I draw a head. You ask
"who's that supposed to be?"
I won't tell you. We laugh
and fall back on the mattress
that's covered with pretty yellow cloth
and out the river flows, out the window
past the railroad and the town,
and the pine forest of this pillow
where there are light brown
beds of moist pine needles
touched by rays of sun.

6.

The birdbath is filled with rainwater
this morning. Inner process is sort of
composed by inspiration today, good
breathing, good flow of blood from the lungs
it's a matter of course
of course, of course
but still has to be guided by mental
arithmetic of some kind, good breathing
while running, running, running
arms back and up and out and reaching
to pull the air back in, and getting there.

7.

Her voice is heard, and then the child's
who is her daughter, and they both sound
very young, they are both young girls
and they are talking in the garden
under the pear trellis, and their
hair shines in the sun, and the pear
petals snow on them, and they are one
person, going down through linear
time, but apart from it, parallel
and talking, and breathing again
and flashing and moving along that line

8.

I interrupt this to go to the store
on the way my soul turns inside out
and drains out through my heels. The air
instead of bathing the sea claws it open
and leaves pieces of color I jog on.
Soft footfalls won't alarm the people
who are planted in sleep, but the dog on
Poplar's roused by even the lightest
pad of sneakers in the dust, and bites.
I growl him off by turning animal myself
and move through the fog swiftly, like a wheel
that breathes

9.

Here you are, and it is dynamite to cohabit
with a jackrabbit. I had to hustle
like The Roadrunner, but now that's over.
Before I take another breath
of the fragrant desert air, the flowery cottonwood,
I want to tell you you are the clearest woman on earth.
I don't mean to speak from the platform of my ego
but from true urgency, like the boy who stood
on the burning deck. It was a state of emergency:
his pants were on fire. With me it is not like that.
I am more interested in an equal
discourse to express my thoughts. I think
the cactus flower's odor is like your skin's.

10.

Imagination, have mercy. Whereupon it
occurs to me kindness or malice might
be spatial. A small room is an actual pain
and I instinctively run for the open.
From the shadows to the light as Duane
Thomas said. An evenness of delight of
horizons that widen at the ocean's edge.
Above the deep blue sky a black unreal
in which a real lies hidden and alive.
It's a song I've heard before. I have
believed I needed to be given something
in order to live, and I was wrong. It
never occurred to me to just go out & take it!

11.

Warm ripe days. The sun floods the ridge with color
before dawn, slowly the reddish light implodes
and before dusk the moon floats up like a softball
over the sea. Starbright glimmers the weather
satellite in a position akin to that of Venus
or is it the skylab people coming down? Mutual
interests unite people on earth and in the sky,
ah and the heart sighs to be so satisfied
it beats against the skin to bespeak love's beauty
and the air brushes past it with a smoothness
borne by zephyrs from somewhere inland like Houston, Tex.
where the days are hard but the nights are long and warm
from various small fires static electricity causes
to crackle in the sheets, and draw up our auras.

12.

Thought is surrounded by a halo
glowing oddly green. Midsummer love
has aphonies, tuned in from zero.
The sheets are crumpled on the bed.
The skin is everywhere and drips.
The skeleton has gone on vacation.
You can hear birds sing in the woods
and the reef is clothed with sable.
A stray diamond may pivot on your neck,
or your knee be grazed by lips;
in the next room, a distant ball game
on the radio.

13.

Finally night falls, and I am snuffed
by a sort of physical abolition
which covers me with a robe of drowsiness
and narrows my purpose until all
I can do is make it up the stairs
into the bedroom where you're undressing.
I lie down & watch you & the whole
day goes away & in its place a place
remains, for me to go to sleep in
where love & vision are the same.
It's like the gift of light to a
blindman, and I thank you for that.

4.

1974-1978

JAPAN

to Reverdy

It rains endlessly and the wind blows a blue light in from the south
A blue cloud broken into arms like a tree and dark
And a spark
Of life glimmered in me
As I climbed up to the roof
Spooning blacktar into the cracks in the moulding
The wind blows buckets of rain in my face
So I scream "fuck!" back into the rain
And the rain scream "fuck!" back at me
And suddenly
I grasp
The problem of life

The solution of the problem of life is the disappearance of this problem

But is it possible to live so that life stops being problematic?

I don't grasp the mechanics

I know how the piston engine works
And I know how the salami
Fits into the purse

I know how to read a box score
For pleasure and I believe life has a meaning
God means understanding the question about the meaning of life
Life has a meaning
All right

The rain keeps falling
And there's a noise in my head
An uncivilized and horrible blaring tone
This is why
Even though I know
The world is given to me

I suspect it is the gift
Of some alien will
This is why
I keep getting the feeling
Only a man who lives in the present is happy
For in life in the present there is no death
There is only a pulled groin muscle
An electric heater
A radio ad for pool tables sale priced at 18.88

Fear in the face of death is the best sign of a false life

Not that it makes you a bad person but

All right
But what
Is this?

Is it the world?

All right

Live happily!

So I look right over
The present
Into the future
Which is about
15 inches in front
Of my face

Campy begins his slide
Striding close to the ground and throwing his legs out in front
His cap falls away
His toe hooks around the bag
And tags it
And some kind of goddam
Hydraulic lift
Picks up the stadium
And tosses it back into history

So that's Time
It does funny things to objects
And people
Are sick of it

They've had enough
It is not a happy world

The only life is the happy life on television and I stop believing it
I stop hearing the radio
I call up the hospital
The amenities of the world are so many graces of fate
All right
Don't change your mind

The body of the beast seeks its elected donut

The louder I yell the louder the wind gets
And so I slap the black caulking
Onto the window moulding
I see my own reflection
In the window
Shrieking
Back at myself

My hood scares me

If the shoe pinches, wear it

Okay
We can only foresee what we ourselves construct
The hydrophobe foresees death by drowning
And by George
Water clogs all his pores
Faster than he can imagine it
So watch out what you do
Or you will wind up
On the muddy bottom

It pours
A hierarchy of drops

What do I know about God and the purpose of life?

A green banana

Ah lovely South America I am coming

I am a person
Of scarce merit
But I will do anything
For a taste of pussy
There you have it
So let me in
Carmen Miranda

I want to be warm & dry
I want to lie
In a hammock holding a cool drink
Reading Conrad

I want to talk to Glenn Beckert

I can make myself independent of fate by putting my fingers in this
    socket and then stepping into this tub of water
But that's the easy way out
The hard way is to go on plowing through the happiness
The goddam no money energy crisis deformed child happiness

Particular objects fly around in the wind
And the green snaking badges of hate break forth
As the storm gets real crude
Ethics and esthetics go up in smoke and

I go looking for my basketball
I find it
And I dribble around
On the bricks

The Feast of the Nativity rushes toward us
Like a tornado
And drops its snout
Into our wallets

Particles of money are sucked up
Into the blue cloud
And arranged in a series

I'm a registered voter
A man of knowledge
Husband and father
Early bird pig chauvinist
Indifferent wrecker of ideologies
What has history got to do with me? Shoo! Scat!

Mine is the first and only world

I want to report how I found the world

I lunged up from the cathedral of fat
Took a bite of the air
Watched and waited and listened
Became my own solipsism made out of gas
Seized up and devoured a molecule from one of God's breasts
And fell dead

Meaning is use
Got that Dwight?
I meant to use this
Friendly pelvis
For a pillow
All my life
But daylight interrupted
And gave these objects shape

The dusky browed ape people we move among
And their chattel
Drifting like mobile bumps
Beneath the ever reaching rain on the spongy horizon

135

The dust lowers on them again and again and again
Like a theatre curtain deployed by a spastic

They are our lookalikes
Be they Cro Magnon or Tierra del Fuegan
From this vantage we cannot really tell
But I can
And do

I crow
Meaningless words
Out into the Open wound
Of the sky
And
The rain streams down my face anyway

You call that life?

I chop some wood
Knowing I'll be able to say
With Reverdy
I lived in a time
When a piece of wood
Or a lump of coal
Was more valuable
Than a nugget of gold
And I wrote in the loft
And the rain
Falling on the dormer window
Became blue

And
Winter hunted me
In the street

And
You can never
Sleep
Once you've opened your eyes

Pierre
I address you
Across
The centuries
That have taken place
Since Nineteen Hundred

You
Like Jonathan Jackson
Were a righteous dude

I salute you
You
With your limpid corolla
Your blinded goldfish
And your broom
That swept away lightening bolts

I am for you the dawn and day intact

Apply this to sounds too

I will conclude my speech
With a few words
On the Arab Oil Embargo

You've probably never heard of that
Because you've been dead for 11 years
And you had all the energy you needed

You hastened to gild yourself with it invisibly, I know

Your loins were big
But you did not know
There was a Dan Ellsberg

He was still plodding in the think tank
When you blew out your last breath

That's OK
Because in your life
You performed an important restitution

You abolished the eternal weight of symbolism
By flying over the gas of the dull canal
On a 747
And for that I thank you

So I'll see ya later
Give me a call in about a hundred years
I'll be glad to talk ta ya then
N rip off a couple more a yr poems
Like I did back in 1965 when I lifted my work DOORS
From yr poems in the *Poètes d'Aujourd-hui* series

Meanwhile
It's getting dark
Back here in civlization
And the Piltdown Man is disappointed with the amenities
Like not enuf gas for weekend skiing

It's still raining and the sun declines
Invisibly in the distance like a brief violet ever unseen that fades

Jesus Creeping God
I grab at the air
And come up with
A bottle of catsup

If suicide is allowed then everything is allowed

Did Pierre Reverdy ever eat a hamburger?
What were his favorite movies
These are the things I want to know
Not whether his misery was on fire
Because in this he resembles me
And is my *semblable*
Due to a sort of demented Buddhism
To which he did not subscribe

And as for me
Forget it

The pen of the universe is stocked with bitching critters
Who gripe about their karma
And want out of the whole hierarchy
And I don't blame them
For I have lied to my fellow Americans
Concerning the sin of suicide
Or is even suicide in itself OK?

Wishing is not acting
And just as I'm about to discover the eternal verities
Luckily
My beautiful wife walks into the room
And leads me by the hand
To the bathroom
In Japan

SINCE VIETNAM

1

You live it forwards, but only understand it backwards:
Life is like that, happily—

It is our only consolation, this darkness
Since Vietnam . . .

And this silence, which absorbs the most eloquent cry without a ripple
As the winter ocean absorbs a brief snowfall.

2

Time goes only in one direction: down through the centuries like a river . . .
At the end the river opens into a broad delta, and then a wide sea, into which
     the ages flow and melt like great blocks of ice . . .
And so the massed events that make up history are dispersed into the
     great oceanic wave of space itself . . .
"The postman always rings twice," it's said, meaning that one's actions
     often flock back to one
Years later in their resurrected form, as meanings; and Vietnam now
     begins to do this . . .

3

The gone ghost of the decade shuffles toward nothing
In self-aversion, comfortable pain

Under cold stars of winter, hard points of light
That shine as expressionlessly as the eyes of the dead.

In Connecticut and Nebraska, wind sings in frozen power lines.
In Ohio, cars have been abandoned up to their windows in drifts, their
     roofs shining in the

Sun like glistening outer bodies of insects in transformation.
Over the Great Slave Lake heaven opens up and down floats irradiated
     metal, a shimmering light.

4

"What's out there?" the people ask.
"Are we alone?"

Under snow, the country becomes itself,
Hugging itself, unwilling to know.

5

After a lost war, the poet said, one should write only comedies;
And we have written these for history with our lives.

January, 1978

5 A.M.

The forest is awake and clicking already
It strains its neck like Bob Clemente
so the treetops can get up as high as they can
and see more of America

*

No sooner have
the first sparks of the burnt out sun
scattered across the rafters of the deflowered landscape
in all their warm silverness
than with brown head burst into itself like a crushed melon
limbs dead
and vision furry
I step into my Keds
and hit the road for my dawn ramble into prehistory

MORNING LEAVES ME SPEECHLESS

Morning leaves me speechless
The road flows into the trees
The sun rises through the leaves
And if I look up through them as I run
Dazzles me till I got to look away

Some miles into the silverness
The road becomes a stream
My Keds swim on like a song
Complete unconsciousness sings

It's like epilepsy
I'm not cold my feet don't hurt I can't remember my name
The cars go by and the drivers wave
I can't remember their names either but it's okay

Fall over?
Are you kidding?
Does a fish fall over?

JANUARY

Sun showers
like tears of joy
between storms;

strong feelings
coming and going
and huge white flying clouds—

out of a blue sky
a sudden downpour
catches the sun unawares.

LOVE (after La Rochefoucauld)

Like ghosts,
  much talked about,
    seldom seen.

REALISM

The smashed weirdness of the raving cadenzas of God
Takes over all of a sudden
In our time. It speaks through the voices of talk show moderators.

It tells us in a ringing anthem, like heavenly hosts uplifted,
That the rhapsody of the pastoral is out to lunch.
We can take it from there.

We can take it to Easy Street.
But when things get tough on Easy Street
What then? Is it time for realism?

And who are these guys on the bus
Who glide in golden hats past us
On their way to Kansas City?

THE BIG CIGARS

It's both never and always a work day for me
I work every day and never get paid
This and putting my pants on one leg at a time
Are two things I have in common with the great geniuses
Einstein, Socrates, Rimbaud
The real heavies of the universe, the big cigars

THE COLOR OF STEPPED ON GUM

is the color of our times.
The light of our times is
the light in the 14th St.
subway at 2 a.m. The air
of our times is the air of the
Greyhound depot, Market
& Sixth. It is prime time. A passed
out sailor sits pitched
forward like a sack of laundry
in a plastic bucket seat
his forehead resting on
the movie of the week. *The Long Goodbye.*

SO LONG

Life with its heart down on its hands and knees
Has wasted so much time and lost
90% of the big ones for so long it's not
Worth it, no, I don't care what you say
                              said the champion

AUTOBIOGRAPHY

In huge leaps of false delight I pursued boredom like a long jumper
never knowing the despair beyond which one must pass
in order to become an ordinary man like Gene Tenace

CRISIS ON THE SAVANNAH

> *"I must complain the cards are ill-shuffled till I have a good hand."*
>
> —Jonathan Swift

"Believing something will happen
   Because I don't want it to
And that some other thing won't
   Because I do—" I wailed to the dealer—

"This is desperation." "Yeah?" he said. But then by
   Your graceful lines, your lioness' mane,
Your heat as you returned from
   Your day in the jungle, you relieved me from

What in myself was desperate,
   What even now insists on wishing
And believing. Still in the sheen of finely-breathing
   Blond hair that covers you,

By the flashing way you move from tree
   To tree, and from room to room,
Making it a bright full house,
   I find at least the light to see the cards I am dealt.

THE CATCH

I threw my youth into the garbage
Where in the furnace of so many intense nights
It was forged into a blade
Which slammed down with a clang
Between me and everything.

I jumped back and forgot everything.
All I can remember now is how
I behold *you*, lost in infinity with *me*,
While I do my art works.

It doesn't make us rich, this life
But it makes us desperate
And get that little catch
In our throats, like having a bird there.

EM INSPIRED BY CERTAIN LINES OF PASTERNAK'S

"Tom has become a very serious person"
—Mary Hartman, Mary Hartman

as into a life that is rarely anything but desperate
only clarity that ever arrives comes from you,
also in January your womanly face like a small secret stream of sorrow
ms the chill river of my being with its frown
t looks like a tired windshield wiper blade
ause it must scrape away all the ice in Siberia

at other times when living sickens more than sickness does itself,
the quality of mercy is strained, a silence cloaks the steppes;
n beauty is still the root of audacity, yes, but laughter
ases razor blades into the chest, causing tiny coronary events
off in Moscow, where Dr. Zhivago kicks the bucket

ny novel your shoes will sleep with everything, nonetheless,
ereas in reality they will merely surround your human feet
to the future, in whose epic snows we will be lost,
at difference will it make whether you had pretty feet
de your snowshoes, or feet at all?

he Hotel Vacancy beneath whose skylights there are no floors to walk
ny years will go by, and then many more,
one long stride to perdition under cold blue starlight
which you are the only blessing, but even you will fall

ny great years will go by and after a while
ll no longer be alive: Think of me Then
en unlike now to open a window does not make you think of jumping out,
begin again without me

LIFE FLOWED BETWEEN US...

Life flowed between us.

It was the voice in the shadows
that flows between the centuries

like dark hair flows
across a pillow.

When I looked,
I knew what it was like
to dip a foot
into the river of forgetfulness.

And the voice said: go ahead.

TO REVERDY, AGAIN

Pierre, I know you are dead and can't
hear me, but permit me a question.
Did you, as your friend Stanislaus Fumet
once said, really stretch your lyricism
from earth to heaven
and back again, like an electrical conductor
lighting up both places?

Somehow I don't think so.
You were no mere messenger.
Communication is too political.
And you detested politics, as
your friend Stanislaus said.
He could never forget, though,
your categorical phrase
about the Resistance—
which you described as "nothing
but de Gaulle!"
                The rest,
you said, was "merely episodic."

Episodes of your own
resistance, your asceticism
and obvious love of privacy
are mostly unknown
because, as you once wrote
on a publisher's bio sheet,
your life was "without interest."
We learn nothing about
what you do every day from your poems,
nor about where you live
or what you look like.
Fumet tells us you were big,
with oily black eyes containing highlights
like a Sarazen's, and a smile
his wife said illuminated everything.

155

It does not, alas, illuminate your biography.

During the war you apparently went
South and lived mostly alone
with your wife and prayed a lot.
Your solitude, which disgusted others,
seemed admirable to Fumet.
He believed your "grandeur"
consisted in "not conceding
a thing to your entourage."
Instead of simply standoffish,
he perceived you to be
passionately *dégagé*.
     Charitable
he may have been, but you?
You were no sweetheart.

"I love to chat with Sartre,"
you told Stanislaus one time
years later—you'd come back to Paris—
"but I hate his book on
Baudelaire. It's as if the man
just committed suicide
in my living room. From
now on, Sartre doesn't exist.
Don't ask me why. His
book just murdered him!"

Then there was Max Jacob,
who converted you to Catholicism
with his convincing parlor replay
of the Passion of Christ, and whom
you later wouldn't say hello to
on the street. Why not, Pierre?

Toward the end there you
spent all your time by
yourself, on your knees praying.
Up at 5:30, no distractions,
the life of the monastery.
Heavy fatigue by night.

"Total Union with God,"
you told Fumet in a letter.
Did it do you any good?
Did it erase the century?

"Ours is an age of art and war,"
Max Jacob remarked 50 years ago,
"And Reverdy is the poet of war."

I'm afraid Max understood your place in the century
better even than your friend Stanislaus Fumet.
The blood was not on your hands
but it is on your pages, Pierre.
Out of it your friend Picasso decocted
the thin red line he used
to illustrate one of your books.
And out of it you distilled a syntax
of terror and doubt, and then
mounted that on a grand
and neutral architecture
of modernity, perhaps false.

In your works you bequeathed a well-lit freeway
that plunges deep into the night of the world.

In your evasive metaphors the anxiety
is like unsentimental music by Poulenc
and the strange desires
are like the irregular heartbeat
of something enormous
hidden under a tarpaulin in the next room.

When I close your book I can hear It breathing
for a second or two
and the feeling puts my life under a shadow for days.

And yet Fumet says you had the fists of a boxer!

TO UNGARETTI

On high the fables blaze.

Giusep', you knew the hard
    Egyptian stars
       twenty years
    before you ever set foot
    on the factual shore
       of that land whose modern poetry
       you were to become
         the father of, Italy

And similarly
   your I
      is grave and slow
    and your longing gains
       on what it longs for
      deliberately
    like a quarter horse, strong
       but not swift,
     taking the thoroughbreds on
       at ten furlongs

You lasted

When you were old and silvery
     you gave Ed Sanders some of your pubic hair
  to deal to the trivia speculators
    to help pay the costs
  of his magazine of poetry
          proving that
     you are more modern than Montale or Robert Lowell

Unlike Ike
     you were able to sustain a hardon
      at an advanced age
    just ask Barbara Guest
      she was standing next to you at the party
    when Ed brought the envelope around

In your poems

your I
        or ego
    is like a rock (speaking of hard)
        or other resistant object
        which your words
                break into
            and/ or excavate
                causing the escape of heat
                via radiation

So that
        reading your works
    is like experiencing
        a series of shocks
    of dead stars
            that exploded
        light years off
                way far out in space
            and transmitted
                only this small signal
                    which
                        "illumines," as
                        you said
                        in the greatest two-
                        word poem
                        in history,
                            "immensity"

That poem is called *Morning*
    and reminds me
        of how sleep is only
            an imitation of dead people

and of how the out-thereness
            of those stars you loved
        can be imported
            into a worldly body
                only by that great smuggler,
                Doctor D

You spent some time with him
            in the trenches
            in 1916
            and in the Isonzo
                where you wrote *The Rivers*
        and then again in 1936
            when Mussolini
                chased you to Brazil
            where your young son
                        was as you wrote
                    in your great poem
                    Tu Ti Spazzasti,
                    "shattered
                            in a blindness
                        as durable
                            as crystal"

Putting together
        these few
            poems that are like
            machines of
        hard and terrible
                    structure
                    came easy
            if you call
                going through all that
                    war and death
                    easy

When I think about you now
        I always remember that
            under the Southern Cross's wild conflagration
                    your father
                    helped build
                        the Suez Canal

160

THE DEATH OF VUILLARD

*"He penetrated ever deeper and deeper into his own
being, always in the same direction."*
                                        —Claude Roger-Marx

In 1938,
            in his last major work,
the enormous mural
      for the Palace of the League
   of Nations at Geneva,
            the old painter, Vuillard,
                  went beyond his range
                        for the first time.
He took on, this master of "intimism"
      and the psychologically appropriate
            interior—before whose
      painting visits
            one of his subjects,
                  Anna de Noailles,
            had commanded her maid, "Hide
                  the vaseline, Monsieur Vuillard
            paints everything he sees!"
—he now took on a theme
      straight out of 19th
            century romantic mythology,
                  a real production number,
            "Peace Protecting the Muses"!

It was an idea straight out of
   that hero of his youth,
Puvis de Chavannes.
                  And it was of Puvis, indeed
that Vuillard often daydreamed
            when, so near death,
                  and perched up high on scaffolding
                  (that this was the method
      of the masters of old
            filled him with pride

161

and anxiety),
             he went toe-to-toe
with fatigue
        and difficulty
of every kind.

The composition was so big
      he could only work on
            one tiny part
                 at a time.
           He worked, and time went by.
Somehow, lost in the bright mythology,
      his hand shaky,
           he painted the whole wall.
  Unfortunately the tiny soul
        of his genius
          had fluttered away from him
              on the tiny butterfly wings
                   of a Titania, in the meantime.
Down floats Peace, gushing her benediction,
             forty feet above our heads.
Only in the colonnade of trees
      in the background,
            recalling the sunlit verdure
                   of his earlier work,
                 do we see the true Vuillard.
The rest is
      jello-flavored Allegory,
             Euterpe leaning on her theorbo
                 and all that—
                 what Vuillard couldn't make up
                      he lifted from Poussin.

Finished, it had the softness
        of an illusion,
      like an idea about Asia
             had by someone in Ohio.
Still, the old man was happy with it.

Maybe to him this invocation

of the immortals
was like reserving
a grandstand seat
in the hereafter.
Or maybe he
was just happy
to have got it over with!

"Was he satisfied?" asks his biographer, at this point.
He was, he was!

He had dreamed so long
with one eye on his work
and the other on the Great Beyond
that now that he had
the gods on the end of his hand
how could he not be happy?
Is it really
an irony
that he who had
dreamed of escaping
his own century
did so by going
backward and turning
into his dream?

And that he escaped
the real in his next
axiom?
Surfboarding into Death?
Because that's what happened next.
After the League of Nations
Doctor D
told him,
Put those
brushes away.
Ever logical, Vuillard
recognized the inevitable
and did just that.

163

He was working on another large decoration
                 in the winter of 1940.
           It was not one of the
                     better winters
                         to be alive in France.
As he worked,
           Vuillard commented to a friend
                     with sad vehemence
           about the errors and weaknesses
                     of his time.
           He said some nasty things about
     Puvis. He put down his old
           ally, Maurice Denis'
                 latest book on religious art.
           "All that stuff sucks!" he shouted.

Vuillard was sitting on a sofa
           at the time. It was an old sofa.
           He, too, was old. He scratched his beard.
                 It was raining. His head was bent back.
           He was old.
                 It was the winter of 1940 in France.
           Suddenly he stopped talking.

TO FRANZ KAFKA

"It is as if I were made of stone, as if I were my own
tombstone, there is no loophole for doubt or for faith, for love
or repugnance, for courage or anxiety, in particular or in
general, only a vague hope lives on, but no better than the
inscriptions on tombstones."

Franz,
  if you'd gone to work
in your family's
    asbestos factory
instead of at
    the insurance institute
you might have become
    a success in business
and stayed away from
    that disastrous literature
which ruined your health
    by keeping you up nights
so that at six each morning
    you had to dress
in your immaculate suit
    and go off to work
with your thin frame and narrow head
    all twisted
from sleeplessness and
    fatigue of the nervous system

But then when I think
about it I realize
  you probably would have had
    your problems at
the asbestos factory too

TO LENNY BRUCE

Lenny,
  ever since the dudes
    who call the shots
    at William Morris
      blew me off the deck
      for leaving all the "fuck's"
      in Mark Fidrych's life story
      I've thought constantly of you

You brought those words everybody says
  out from under the counter
  of the business club
    and the Kiwanis luncheon
      and for that I thank you

You said, *Fuck* that secrecy
  and for that
    got slapped down
  by "society"
      which is just a name
      for that great spiritual Milwaukee
        the entertainment business dreams up
        and calls America
It feared you
          because you weren't embarrassed
          to tell the truth

In the end, all your high class fans—
  your Nat Hentoff types, your Dusty Hoffmans—
    where were *they*
  when you lay face down in vomit
      on the bathroom floor
        with the police photographer standing over you
      changing his flashbulbs
          and wondering about his breakfast?

Did you mind it,
or was it just too late to matter?

And did the royalty they got
off their articles and movies
pick you up off the bathroom floor
and wipe your face with a washrag
and put breath back in your mouth
so you could live again to talk dirty another day?

HOW I BROKE IN

Introduction

I had my coat off and my sleeves rolled up, but the door was
too hot to rest an arm on. A horse dozed under a clump of live
oaks. A brown Mexican sat on the ground and ate something
out of a newspaper. Tumbleweed rolled across the road and
came to rest against a granite outcrop. A lizard that had been
there an instant before disappeared without seeming to move
at all. The guy stopped the car and told me to get out.
  "This is as far as I can take you Pal."

1.

"But how far do I have to go?"
He shook his head and pushed me out the door
With eyes as blue as the sky
And as big as all Utah.
The wind hummed *Mood Indigo*
As he left me in a cloud of dust,
Rubbing my eyes
And checking my manuscript book.
I walked as far as Truth or Consequences.
The wind bit and stung me.
Bugs bit into my skin.
The desert was wide, quiet.
I saw it as a job.
I kept on walking.

2.

Human beings are joined together by ropes pulled tight
Over the void. If the tension of these ropes is reduced
A single human being slips and it is a bitter thing
To see him dangle, like a spiritual Ehrlichman,
Twisting in the wind. But even worse, if around one
Person the tension grows too great and the rope breaks,
That person falls to a fate worse than any briar patch.
That is why we should always hold tight to
The ambient ones! For via this enmeshment we possess
Immunity to Snuff! Yet our grasp should be light.
I incline to the belief that because girls are so light
They sustain us. They do it because they are so light.
That is why we have to love the girls and why
They should love us. And we have to hold them lightly!

3.

It just makes sense that way. Few things do, these days.
When there are books around, it's even fewer.
My God, I could be happy without books.
If we had no books, and needed some, we could
Simply write them! Right there and then!
But not until we needed them. And then
They would have to be books that affect you
Like being kissed by your sister
And catching the kissing disease, and kissing
Her again and again, and getting sicker and sicker,
But liking it more and more each time, and in time
Not being able to do without it, and letting its
Presence or absence rule your day. And when
You pass away of it, leaving it everything.

4.

Candy came and poured the Cokes
And from then on it was all a dream
Just like the other day on the Main Line
When my fingers danced across the keys.
But when I'm done I don't read my writing
I wash it down with forgetfulness and a poem
I have a beautiful home
A beautiful wife and a beautiful sales record
And if this pickup truck stops
And lets me out under the stars of the desert night
I'll walk into Truth or Consequences
Half tight and looking back inside my head
For your blue eyes as big as all of Utah
Humming *Mood Indigo* how far do I have to go

5.

To find you? Do I have to run long? I hear you
Talking in the pounding of my own feet on the sand and want to shoot myse
I take my coat off, roll my sleeves up
I write in my notebook, I want to shoot myself because of you
But Truth or Consequences looms up large
Before me, familiar, like a book of mine
My books run long
What I need right now more than my books is a ride into Malibu
I start running along the side of the road in the sand
The blood is pounding on a door in my head
The little man won't let it in
He is too old, he is too tired, he doesn't understand it
I fall asleep before a broad tract of sand and surf
In my sleep I grow heavier

170

6.

I am filled with a light, pleasant quiver
That persuades me of abilities
I can convince myself even now
That I do not possess
All the same, at this moment
Even their nonexistence
Is enough to fill me with happiness
It's like seeing a large log in the snow
And knowing you can roll it
And going up to it and trying it
And not being able to do it
And knowing it doesn't matter
All my sentences are perfect
Even if they crumble in my hands

7.

Every word scans the horizon
Hoping another word won't approach and qualify it
Across those broad tracts of surf and sand
Between here and Truth or Consequences
Those girls are light
They have light bodies
They sustain us as we go out to make another dollar
Along the Main Line
Where I go into my brain
Like you would go into your office
To do your work of the day
One by one my perfect sentences pile up
Like logs in the sand
I try to roll them but they won't budge

8.

What's the song say, roll me like a wheel?
That's a job for a psychiatrist
I have a sinus headache from watching The Captain & Tennille Show
I scan the horizon for words to qualify life
Find none
And end up living it
Like I would have done if I hadn't gone on this road trip
My feet pounding on the sand
Augment my existence
And it's like hearing you say
I wish you were some good, you're smart but you're no good, Frank
I'm no good, but I love you, I say
I'm not much good, Cora, but I love you
God damn you then, you say, scratch my back

9.

There is no compensation in baseball
That's the new free agent rule
I'm having a Big Mac attack
We do it all for you
The idea was, she never had seen Malibu
She wanted to cut over on this back road to the beach
And then turn around and drive back up to Santa Barbara
It was all a plot to bump off her main squeeze
They would squeeze each other's bodies
Until he was like to break her neck
He was a big man, 6'4, maybe 6'5
She called him Dan
Even though his name was Maurice
He said I will die now but come alive later in your memory

10.

I cross five lines out for every one that gets by me
Franz Kafka did that too
So did the hero of *Le Feu Follet*
And riding back on recollection's vector
I come to a reading at Trinity College in 1963 or 4
And a poem of Anselm Hollo's
About writing a great work in a transport of heat and rapture
And then going back over it
In the cold light of morning
And one by one crossing out every line until not even the title is left
Anselm's hero survived it with nothing worse than a hangover
But the hero of *Le Feu Follet* put a gun in his mouth at the end
And Franz Kafka died of laryngeal tuberculosis
Zeno, pressed as to whether anything is at rest, said yes, the arrow rests
                                          while it is flying

11.

In my sleep I have greater weight
Distance holds the life firm
In tranquility, closeness sets fire to it
The clarity of all these events
Makes them mysterious
Just as the dependable horizon of a fence
Rests the eye
As it roams across the surf's broad tracts
And yet inspires inadequate respect in us
And there the sentence hangs itself up
It's a suspended sentence
Until it's up we can't leave the state
Her eye was all black, her breasts were not drawn up
And pointing at me, but soft, and spread out in two pale splashes

173

12.

She said, Rip me, Frank
So Dan stripped all her clothes off
She squirmed, but slow
So they'd slip out from under her
A fog came over Maurice
His brain went away from him
And nested in a far off land
She fixed two drinks
One for her and Frank
And one for Dan
And then she closed her eyes
And threw back her head
And Maurice went down on her
Far off in Prague Franz Kafka was writing *Amerika*

13.

We had a big blow-off
I turned the radio on
The Sheriff stuck his penis into a package of Bull Durham
And it was good
But I had my face in the foxhole at the time
And didn't understand his meaning
As he sang
The words came out sweet and slow
I turned off the radio
God kissed us on the forehead
And then a big airplane took her off into the sky
Even though the plane moved, it was at rest
Her body was light and portable
I refilled her glass and lit us both cigarettes

14.

Franz and Dan and Maurice and Frank left the driving to us
And took the bus into Truth or Consequences
It was the end of the long road trip to the Crab Nebula
In my head the blood pounded
I looked at her
She still had sand on her clothes
I brushed some of it off
The touch re-aroused me
There was a little light far off in the distance
It was her bare throat
A magic hand closed around it and threw her down on the sand
At that moment across the prairie
There drifted the first notes of an étude by Brahms
Just as the hand touched the keys the wild stars all vanished

15.

Over the dead mesa the sun was uplifted
Dan dunked his donut in a cup of blood
And in my head I saw the story go by over and over
I couldn't stand it
I sat down and drew up a list of possible lucky stars
Where Zeno's arrow might have landed
After speeding errantly off the bow of a shocked Maurice
The negative alone, however strong, could not convince him
To return to the sanitorium
After one kiss from her lips
Franz fell into a fit of frantic vomiting
The had to drag the poor fellow away
In his insurance office they spoke softly and felt sorry for him
Martin Buber pulled his pants down and spanked him twice on his pale little ass
Once on each cheek

175

16.

My prose I find just as tiresome as my poems for the same reason
My feet I hear pounding under me in the sand
My fingers fly over the keys of the typewriter on Zeno's airplane
My plans for books go up in smoke
My sentences flop through the air like inflated pigskins
A dim figure gallops toward me across the plain
It turns out to be Harvey Martin
He is looking for a sack
It is no fond thing he intends to do
It is a thing full of gore and jeopardy
For this cowboy of whom we speak
Is a gigantic tube of skin
Into which you could squeeze two of Sir John Suckling
The time has come for me to say the Long Goodbye

17.

The Long Goodbye
Tells of a simple woman
Who had six husbands
Two million dollars
And one toe too many
And of the surgery she underwent
At the Mayo Clinic
During the course of which
A small but very cold finger
Crawled the whole length of her spine
Like a frozen insect
Operated by a tiny motor
That was last used in 1913
To drag Kafka's pen across the first page of *Amerika*

18.

ast colorless and uncluttered sky as big as all Utah
1 I stepped off a bus in West Hollywood
1 got tangled up in that sky so like the movies
atly inspired I wrote and had printed my own book
1 then lost myself in the pursuits of the cowboys
 after five years of constant eating drinking and sex
: lack of philosophical reflection staled my mind
adaches, insomnia, grey hair and despair arrived all at once
solved to return to my home at any price
ore it was too late I rode the long way over the hills
1 on my first sight of it I fell and kissed the rain-soaked ground
 of which I had been born and to which I will return
1 across which, in my web of folly and pain,
w stride to the neighborhood drugstore to purchase beaver magazines and Excedrin

19.

he morning I look into a Monument Valley
inted eighteen months ago
h a new clarity I had only lately acquired
1 then I rub my eyes
1 check my smokes
1 off I go to the soda shop
ere Candy came and poured me Cokes and pouted
le I glimpsed her ass
ler the light blue waitress uniform
1 outside the sky as big as all Utah smiled
1 Candy smiled at me and I smiled
1 we went out back
1 I got blood on my lip
m where I bit it during

20.

Then later we did our homework together
And Dan and Frank came over with a six pack
And we all ate granola bars
And talked about the old days back at the Mayo Clinic
And listened to the big airplanes go by
And held our breaths
And talked about and wrote and read great books
And Candy came and poured us Cokes
And that filled up our tanks with sugar
And sustained us
And that is why we loved us and the girls
And held them tightly
Like we held our private manuscript books
Into which we wrote our secret poetry notes about wanting to shoot ourselves

21.

It was an enormous morning
I stuck out my thumb
Humming *Mood Indigo* and looking for a dollar
To fall out of the blue sky
Containing Immunity to Snuff
In which I twist like a spiritual Ehrlichman
Until someone reduces the tension of these ropes
With which the girls hold us
And the first thing that went by
A pickup truck driven by a girl that looked just like my sister
Stopped and picked me up
She said, I know you, you're the famous writer
I said, I'm no good, but I would love to eat you up
It worked out fine until I had a Big Mac attack near Malibu

22.

I pressed her bodies together tightly then
The way they pressed Zeno
About whether anything was at rest
And her firm breasts
Fixed two drinks
And then her mind floated away
And I shifted her dress
And she threw back her eyes
And closed her head
And said, Rip me Frank
I reminded her I was Dan
And that Frank wouldn't be over until later
And that, frankly, I didn't mind
If he never got here

23.

Far off in Prague, however, I turned the radio on
To get my mind off things
I had my face in a foxhole at the time
And my penis in a package of Bull Durham
The blood pounded in my head
A fog came over my airplane
I saw Candy's inflated throat
It looked like it was made of pigskin
Her clothes still had sand on them
Harvey Martin's footsteps were getting close
The sun was dropping down into a cup of blood over the dead mesa
And the Truth or Consequences bus was pulling up
I stuck out my thumb and stepped aboard
Dan swung on after me and the next thing I knew we were both in pictures

Printed September 1978 in Santa Barbara & Ann Arbor
for the Black Sparrow Press by Mackintosh and Young
& Edwards Brothers Inc. This edition is published
in paper wrappers; there are 200 hardcover copies
numbered & signed by the author; & 26 lettered
copies have been handbound in boards by Earle Gray,
each with an original drawing by Tom Clark.

Photo: Gerard Malanga

Tom Clark was born (1941) and raised in the Chicago area, went to school there, worked as a ballpark usher, left for college in the late 50s; took a degree at Ann Arbor (where he won two Hopwood awards); spent four years in England (two at Cambridge on a Fulbright, two at the U. of Essex, teaching, studying and writing poems); edited several magazines, including (for ten years) the poetry section of *The Paris Review;* traveled in Europe and North Africa; returned in 1966 to the U.S., explored New York for a year, then married and moved West; brought up a daughter in a seaside village in Northern California, where he lived for ten years, produced twelve books of poems, three novels, four books on baseball, an opus on the life and times of Damon Runyon, and several hundred paintings and drawings. He now resides with his family in a small town high in the Colorado Rockies.